vegetarian
food for kids

vegetarian
food for kids

Laura Washburn

phototgraphy by Kate Whitaker

RYLAND
PETERS
& SMALL

LONDON NEW YORK

Senior Designer Megan Smith
Senior Commissioning Editor Julia Charles
Head of Production Patricia Harrington
Art Director Leslie Harrington
Publishing Director Alison Starling

Food Stylist Sunil Vijayakar
Prop Stylist Liz Belton
Indexer Hilary Bird

First published in 2011
by Ryland Peters & Small
20–21 Jockey's Fields
London WC1R 4BW
and
Ryland Peters & Small, Inc.
519 Broadway, 5th Floor
New York NY10012
www.rylandpeters.com

10 9 8 7 6 5 4 3 2 1

Printed in China

Text © Laura Washburn 2011
Design and photographs © Ryland Peters
& Small 2011

ISBN: 978 1 84975 142 1

A CIP record for this book is available from
the British Library.

US Library of congress cataloging-in-
publication data has been applied for.

AUTHOR'S ACKNOWLEDGEMENTS
I would like to thank all the friends who happily
discussed their children's favourite vegetarian
foods and recipes as well as the children who
willingly taste-tested my concoctions. Thanks
also to Dr Helen Crawley for nutritional advice,
and for sharing her vegetarian family food
diary with me.

NOTES
• Cheeses started with animal rennet are not
suitable for vegetarians so read food labelling
careful and check that the cheese you buy is
made with a non-animal (microbial) starter.
Traditional Parmesan is not vegetarian so we
recommend a vegetarian hard cheese (such as
Gran Moravia which has the same texture so is
ideal for grating) or Parma (a vegan product).
• All spoon measurements are level, unless
otherwise specified.
• All eggs are medium, unless otherwise
specified. It is generally recommended that
organic free-range eggs be used. Uncooked
or partially cooked eggs should not be served
to the very young, the very old, those with
compromised immune systems, or to women
who are pregnant.
• When a recipe calls for the grated zest/peel of
citrus fruit, buy unwaxed organic fruit and wash
well before using. If you can find only treated
fruit, scrub well in warm soapy water and rinse
before using.
• Ovens should be preheated to the specified
temperature. Recipes in this book were tested
using a regular oven. If using a fan-assisted
oven, follow the manufacturer's instructions
for adjusting your oven's temperatures

contents

building a healthy diet

Vegetables have never been hugely popular with my children, so it is not without a large degree of irony that I find myself writing about cooking vegetarian food for children. This occurred because my then 10-year-old daughter one day announced, out of the blue, that she had become vegetarian. The week prior to this shock revelation had been spent cooking prolifically to stock the freezer with all manner of carnivorous meals as I had an impending deadline and knew time for meal preparation was about to become scarce. My daughter however was firm in her commitment and could not be persuaded to postpone the change for a few weeks, until my deadline passed. The question then became: what in the world was I going to feed her?

I found myself in a very unusual position of not actually knowing what to cook. There is no shortage of vegetarian cookbooks, but I found them all very grown-up and not especially family friendly. I was also concerned for her nutritional welfare. I am not a nutritionist, I am a cook and, while I understand the basics of providing a healthy diet for all those living under my roof, I did not really know how to provide adequately for a vegetarian child. The task before us was daunting. I needed to learn about feeding vegetarian children, as well as find inspiration for meals to cater for my meat-eating family members, while my daughter needed to learn to eat things previously scorned.

The result is this book. I have learned a great deal about the nutritional basics of a vegetarian diet, and they are surprisingly straightforward. What has proved more challenging, is offering meals that appeal to young palates and work in a mixed environment of vegetarians and non-vegetarians – all of the recipes in this book have been conceived with this common contradiction very much in mind. While no meat is used in this book, most of these recipes can be served with simply grilled, stir-fried or roasted meat, poultry or fish, as desired, to offer meals that cater to everyone.

OFFERING VARIETY

This has to be the first stop when thinking about eating well. Regardless of any lifestyle choice, the most important aspect of a healthy diet is variety. It is very easy to fall into a rut of the same foods on a limited cycle of repetition, especially when time for cooking and shopping is short. I did not grow up in a house where we had 'Meatloaf Mondays', but I do understand the attraction of simply repeating a few tried and tested favourites. I can recall a certain regularity of meals from my childhood and I am guilty of perpetuating this myself when pressed for time. The reality for most families is that time is never plentiful so variety is not the easy option. It is important however to vary the foods on offer to ensure adequate nutrient intake. Cooking with seasonal ingredients is one way to achieve this, with cost-saving benefits as well, and trying different dishes from world cuisines is another. Approached this way, escaping the rut feels less of a challenge and more of an adventure. After all, variety is the spice of life, quite literally!

THE BASICS OF GOOD NUTRITION

Current guidelines for a healthy diet include recommendations for high levels of fruit and vegetable intake, reduced saturated fats (found mainly in animal products) and increased wholegrain consumption. All of this is very compatible with a vegetarian diet and most vegetarian children should have good fruit and vegetable intake, which is a real bonus. Removing meat from the diet must involve replacing meat-based nutrients with plant-based nutrients. Deficiencies are the main concern for any parent of a vegetarian child, and on the following pages is a list of the key nutrients and their vegetarian sources.

Opposite: Including a wide variety of different fruits and vegetables daily is essential for a healthy and balanced vegetarian diet.

Protein

When meat goes out the window, there is a host of alternative options:

Pulses and legumes These include peas, lentils and beans, as well as peanuts. In addition to being a good source of protein, many pulses are also high in other important nutrients such as iron, zinc and calcium.

Chick peas/garbanzo beans, kidney beans, lentils, lima beans, cannellini beans, soya/soy beans (edamame), pinto beans, split peas

Meat substitutes Many food manufacturers offer meat substitutes available in the form of sausages, spreads, mince, burgers, etc. Some are made partly from tofu (a soya-based product), some include textured vegetable protein (TVP) and some are made from other vegetable sources, such as Quorn (see also page 13). All of these products can contribute to protein in the diet, but as they are processed foods they should be used alongside other vegetarian protein sources.

Dairy Eggs, milk and cheese, of course, and these are very easy to integrate into a child's diet. So easy, in fact, that dairy can quickly dominate. It is important to remember that large amounts of dairy are not required to offer large amounts of protein; small amounts are sufficient to meet nutritional needs. As a newcomer to vegetarian cooking, I found it difficult to resist the temptation to top everything with grated cheese. The solution, I discovered, was to alternate Western with Asian-inspired dishes and the temptation, and endless cheese, diminished. Again, a great source of protein, to be used in moderation.

Nuts, seeds and wholegrains These are good sources of protein and can be relied on heavily, since there is so much variety on offer in this category. In addition to protein, these foods are a good source of essential fats (also called 'omegas') and contribute to zinc, calcium and iron intake.

Barley, brown rice, buckwheat, millet, oatmeal, quinoa, rye, wheat germ, spelt, wild rice, almonds, cashews, filberts, pumpkin seeds, sesame seeds, sunflower seeds, walnuts

Fruit and vegetables The following are also a good source of protein, when served as part of a varied diet.

Artichokes, beetroot/beets, broccoli, Brussels sprouts, cabbage, cauliflower, cucumbers, aubergine/eggplant, green peas, green (bell) pepper, kale, lettuce, mushrooms, mustard green, onions, potatoes, spinach, tomatoes, turnip greens, watercress, yams, apple, banana, cantaloupe, grape, grapefruit, honeydew melon, orange, papaya, peach, pear, pineapple, strawberry, tangerine, watermelon

Iron

The issue with iron in a vegetarian diet is not that plant-based foods are lacking in this nutrient, it is simply more difficult to absorb iron from plant sources. The result is an emphasis on ensuring high levels of iron-rich food consumption. This is not difficult to achieve by following a varied diet, which includes the

Opposite: Wholegrain foods are nutritious but when serving to children, they must be organic, to ensure pesticide levels are minimized.

following iron-rich foods: dried beans and peas, cereals, whole grains, dark leafy greens, lentils and dried fruit. To help with iron absorption, include Vitamin-C rich foods such as cabbage, broccoli, strawberries, tomatoes and citrus fruit, and include these at the same time as the iron-rich foods.

Vitamin B12

Animal products are the main source of this nutrient. This includes dairy so B12 is more of an issue for vegans than vegetarians. For this reason, be sure to include dairy in your child's diet. Other sources include fortified yeast extract, cereals and sunlight on the skin.

Zinc

As with iron, this is more difficult for the body to absorb from plant-based foods. Zinc is present in wholegrains, pulses/legumes soya products, nuts, wheatgerm and cheese.

Amino Acids

There was a time when it was thought that the best way for vegetarians to ensure an adequate balance of amino acids, the building blocks of protein, was to combine grains with beans or pulses (think beans and rice). Current guidelines suggest that this combining is no longer as vital as previously thought. A variety of plant proteins consumed over the course of one day should provide sufficient essential amino acids.

EAT A RAINBOW

Even armed with a few simple nutrition basics, it can still be daunting to adapt a child's diet to something that, while now more widely accepted, is still outside the mainstream in the Western world. One very good way to get variety and, hence, nutrients, into a vegetarian child's diet is to conceive of each meal plate as a 'rainbow plate'. This is not a scientific formula, but it is a good guiding principle. Simply try to make sure each meal contains a balance of different coloured foods and you can be sure that the nutrient quantities will be well balanced. For example, a monochromatic meal might consist of a jacket potato, bread and butter, yogurt and a banana. All perfectly good options

on their own but, in combination, not ideal. However, a meal of rice with houmous, some carrot sticks and cherry tomatoes, yogurt and green grapes is just as simple and offers a better nutritional balance.

VEGETARIAN FOOD PYRAMID

By far the simplest method I found for providing a balanced vegetarian diet is to follow the guidelines for a Vegetarian Food Pyramid from the American Dietetic Association. Essentially this involves offering foods in quantities represented on a pyramid diagram, starting at the base with the largest emphasis on grains, followed by pulses/legumes, nuts and other protein-rich foods, then vegetables, fruits with fats at the top of the pyramid in the smallest proportion.

PORTION SIZES

A frequent concern for parents is 'are my children eating enough of the right foods?'. More often than not, they probably are if they are not exhibiting any unusual health problems. It is important to remember that children do not always need, proportionally, as much food as adults do. However, almost every rule has an exception and I've found that during growth spurts, including adolescence, children seem to require very large portions.

ORGANIC FOODS

Food from organic agriculture is not reserved for vegetarians alone, nor does a vegetarian diet imply the products must be organic. The evidence as to the health benefits of organic food is inconclusive but this must not detract from the other benefits to be gained from organic foods. Where organic food is relevant to a vegetarian diet, and especially vegetarian children, is in consideration of wholegrains, and in fruit and vegetable peels or skins. Wholegrains have more of the grain intact, which includes the outer surfaces. Non-organically grown wholegrains will have been exposed to more pesticides and other chemicals than organically grown. Because more of the wholegrain plant is

Opposite: Nuts, seeds and wholegrains are good sources of protein and can be relied on heavily since there is so much variety in this category.

intact, so are more of the pesticides, potentially. Organic food cannot be completely free of pesticides, as these are present in the environment, but it will have lower levels of pesticides. Children have smaller body mass than adults and are thus more susceptible to levels of anything they may consume. As there is more nutrition present in wholegrain foods, it makes sense to offer these to children, however it also makes sense to ensure all wholegrain foods are organic to ensure pesticide levels are minimized. For this same reason, I prefer to choose organic produce whenever possible, and when I do, I rarely peel unless absolutely necessary. Organic produce is often more expensive, so it is not always an option but, as a guide, I try to always use at least organic carrots, apples and potatoes if nothing else.

MEAT SUBSTITUTES

In a largely carnivorous culture, such as ours, meals tend to be organized around a central item, which generally involves meat. As a newcomer to vegetarian food, it seemed that tofu, or other soya based products, are often offered as a subsitute. While these are an adequate source of protein, they should not be relied on as a sole source of protein. Variety is a very important part of maintaining a healthy diet and many of these products are very easy and convenient to use, but they should be offered in conjunction with other vegetarian protein sources. In other words, veggie sausages and mince are quick and simple and they tick the protein box, but in the interest of a varied diet, they should be offered in moderation. The variety of soya and other meat-replacement products can be confusing, especially when shifting to a vegetarian diet, so here is a simple breakdown of the different ingredients on offer.

Tofu This often features in vegetarian cuisine. It is high in protein, so it is a good 'meat substitute', if that is how you want to think of it, and it also tends to be served in a 'centrepiece' fashion, like meat. Tofu is simply coagulated soya milk, much like cheese is coagulated cows' milk. There are many different kinds of tofu available: regular, silken, pressed, smoked and marinated, to name a few. In this book, I have used primarily regular and silken tofu. The tofu repertoire is vast and the recipes here are intended merely as an introduction.

A tip passed on by a vegetarian friend, when I expressed my displeasure with using tofu for the first time, was about pressing regular tofu before you use it. Tofu is a very watery thing and the water will escape during cooking, rendering your dish diluted and less tasty. To avoid this, press it before use. This will also help it to absorb any marinade flavours you may use, so be sure to press well before marinating as well (see page 94).

Seitan This is sometimes confused with tofu, as the appearance is similar and it is often sold in the refrigerated section, like tofu. In cooking, seitan can be used much like tofu (stir-fried or added to soups) but it is actually made from gluten. It has a firm and slightly chewy texture and a neutral flavour that, like tofu, benefits from marinating. Some love it, others do not!

Tofu mince Commonly known as TSP: textured soya protein in the UK or TVP: textured vegetable protein in the US , this ingredient does not appear in any of the recipes in this book. It is made from soya flour, is a highly processed ingredient and therefore unnecessary, in my opinion, given the wide and appealing range of plant-based protein foods available.

Quorn This is a brand name for a form of food protein, made mainly from mycoproteins, which was developed in England in the late 1960s. A mycoprotein is a fungus, which sounds unappealing, but remembering that mushrooms are also a member of the fungi family brings this back into the realm of the palatable. It began simply as Quorn cubes for use in home cooked meals, but the range now encompasses a host of different food products, from cooking ingredients to ready-to-eat 'deli' foods. Using Quorn is a reasonable and convenient option when pressed for time, but processed foods are never the healthiest option for children when salt and fats are taken into consideration so use sparingly.

Opposite: Try to make sure each meal you serve contains a balance of different coloured foods and you can be sure that the nutrient quantities will be well balanced.

13

breakfasts

Get your children off to a healthy start in the morning with these easy and nutritious pancakes. They are delicious served simply with a little melted butter and a drizzle of maple syrup, but you can also vary this basic recipe by adding fresh berries, banana, nuts or dried fruit to the batter just before cooking.

multigrain pancakes

**120 g/¾ cup wholemeal/
  whole-wheat flour**

65 g/½ cup oatbran

**85 g/1½ cups plain/
  all-purpose flour**

45 g/¼ cup cornmeal

1 teaspoon baking powder

**½ teaspoon bicarbonate
  of soda/baking soda**

a pinch of fine sea salt

400 ml/1¾ cups milk

2 eggs

2 tablespoons vegetable oil

MAKES ABOUT 15 PANCAKES

Put all of the dry ingredients in a mixing bowl. Whisk together the milk, eggs and oil in a separate bowl or jug/pitcher.

Pour the milk mixture onto the flour mixture and beat until blended but still a little lumpy.

Heat a large non-stick frying pan/skillet and wipe or brush lightly with vegetable oil. Add a ladleful of the pancake batter. Cook until bubbles just appear on the surface then turn over and cook for 1–2 minutes on the other side. Repeat until all of the batter has been used.

Serve immediately with butter and maple syrup, fruit coulis or jam.

WHOLEGRAINS

Wholegrains are exactly as their name suggests; grains such as wheat, barley, rye and oats that are 'whole', in that they contain all three parts of the grain. They are unprocessed, so the outer shell remains intact, unlike refined grains which have been stripped of their germ and bran, making them less nutritious. Wholegrains are a good source of iron and zinc, both important nutrients for vegetarian children.

Here is a delicious and wholesome way to start the day, ideal if there is going to be a long break before lunch. Sliced bread tends to be thin but if using bread from a whole loaf, you may need to add a bit more milk to ensure there is enough; the thicker the bread, the more of the eggy batter it will soak up. Tart red eating apples are the best variety here, but golden delicious are also good. If you are using organic apples there is no need to peel them.

cinnamon french toast with brown sugar, apples & sultanas

2 eggs

4 tablespoons milk

a pinch of sugar

½–1 teaspoon ground cinnamon, to taste

unsalted butter and vegetable oil, for cooking

4 slices organic wholemeal/ whole-wheat bread

FOR THE APPLES

2–3 tablespoons sultanas/ golden raisins

3 tablespoons butter

1 teaspoon vegetable oil

1 large apple, coarsely chopped

1 generous tablespoon dark soft brown sugar

TO SERVE (OPTIONAL)

2–3 tablespoons finely chopped nuts, such as hazelnuts, almonds or pecans

maple syrup or honey

plain Greek yogurt

SERVES 2–3 CHILDREN

First prepare the apples. If the sultanas/golden raisins are not plump, soak them in a small bowl of boiling water for a few minutes. Drain and set aside.

Put the butter and oil in a small non-stick frying pan/skillet and heat until just sizzling. Add the apple pieces and sugar, stir to coat and cook for 8–10 minutes, stirring occasionally, until just tender and lightly browned all over. Add the sultanas/golden raisins after 5 minutes cooking time. Set aside.

Whisk together the eggs, milk, sugar and cinnamon in a shallow dish, until well blended.

Heat the butter and oil together in a non-stick frying pan/skillet large enough to hold at least 2 slices of bread side by side. While the butter is heating, dip a slice of bread in the egg mixture, pricking it lightly with a fork to help absorption.

Turn carefully and soak the other side. Transfer quickly to the heating pan. Repeat for the other slice. Cook over medium-high heat for 2–3 minutes, until well browned, then turn and cook the other sides for a further 2–3 minutes. Transfer to a plate. Add a bit more butter and oil to the pan, and repeat the dipping and cooking for the remaining 2 bread slices.

To serve, cut the bread in half. Divide the apple mixture between the plates, mounding it on top of the bread. Sprinkle with the nuts and serve, with maple syrup or honey and a dollop of Greek yogurt, if liked.

Variation Replace the apple slices with bananas that have been sliced into rounds. Cook as for the apples.

This recipe is a blueprint for smoothie making. Essentially you need fruit – fresh or frozen – or both, a dairy ingredient and a juice. Within that, there is plenty of room for variation. Dairy-free smoothies are also very good, and non-dairy drinks like soya milk, rice milk and even almond milk are fantastic smoothie ingredients. Or simply forgo the dairy altogether and make a fruit and juice smoothie. Just about any fruit you can imagine is good for smoothies. In addition to the fruit suggested here, others such as kiwi, watermelon, cherry, blackberry and mango are especially suitable. Flavour can also be varied by using different juices, just be sure to choose pure juice, not juice drinks which contain added sugar.

strawberry orange yogurt smoothie

250 ml/1 cup plain yogurt
**200 g/1 cup fresh or frozen
    strawberries**
125 ml/½ cup orange juice

SERVES 2 CHILDREN

Put all the ingredients in a blender or food processor and mix until very smooth. Add more juice if a thinner consistency is preferred; add more yogurt or fruit for a thicker consistency. Pour into glasses and serve immediately.

Variations (same method as above unless otherwise specified)

Tropical 1 small ripe banana, broken into a few pieces, mango yogurt and pineapple juice.

Carrot Pineapple 2 small ripe bananas, broken into a few pieces, lemon yogurt, carrot juice and add 125 ml/½ cup pineapple juice.

Orchard Smoothie 1 small ripe banana, broken into a few pieces, peach yogurt, apricot nectar.

Apple Vanilla 1 small ripe banana, broken into a few pieces, vanilla yogurt, pressed apple juice.

Purple Smoothie 1 small ripe banana, broken into a few pieces, fresh or frozen blueberries, blueberry or raspberry yogurt, red grape or pomegranate juice.

Peanut Butter Banana 1 small ripe banana, broken into a few pieces, 2–3 tablespoons smooth peanut butter, plain or vanilla yogurt, milk in place of the juice, 1 tablespoon honey.

These are intended as a breakfast offering, so they contain a high percentage of wholemeal flour and are not as sweet as a dessert muffin. They are nonetheless easy on the palate, and even better spread with cream cheese. Combine with a piece of fresh fruit or some yogurt to round out the meal, or enjoy on their own as a nutritious bite on the run, in a lunchbox or as an after-school snack.

apple & raisin breakfast muffins

**60 g/⅓ cup plain/
all-purpose flour**

**160 g/1 cup wholemeal/
whole-wheat flour**

**110 g/½ cup packed dark
soft brown sugar**

**1 teaspoon bicarbonate
of soda/baking soda**

½ teaspoon baking powder

**1 teaspoon ground
cinnamon**

½ teaspoon ground allspice

a pinch of fine sea salt

**250 ml/1 cup plain yogurt,
milk or buttermilk**

**3 tablespoons organic
rapeseed oil**

1 egg

4 tablespoons honey

100 g/⅔ cup raisins

**1 small tart organic apple,
cored and grated**

1 teaspoon vanilla extract

a 9- or 12-hole muffin tin/pan,
lined with paper cases

**MAKES 9 LARGE MUFFINS OR
12 MEDIUM MUFFINS**

Preheat the oven to 200ºC (400ºF) Gas 6.

Put the plain/all-purpose flour, wholemeal flour, sugar, bicarbonate of soda/baking soda, baking powder, cinnamon, allspice and salt in a large mixing bowl and stir to combine.

Mix the yogurt, oil, egg and honey in a separate mixing bowl and beat until well blended. Stir in half the raisins, apple and vanilla extract.

Pour the yogurt mixture into the flour mixture and mix to combine. Divide between the paper cases, filling them almost to the top. Sprinkle the remaining raisins on top of each muffin. Bake in the preheated oven for 25–35 minutes, until puffed and just brown around the edges. Let cool before serving. These muffins will keep for 2–3 days if stored in an airtight container.

Variation For Nutty Apple Carrot Muffins add 1 small carrot, grated, and 4 tablespoons ground nuts such as almonds or hazelnuts, or 60 g/½ cup chopped nuts such as walnuts or pecans.

RAPESEED OIL
This is one of the lowest in saturated fats of all the vegetable oils. It is a good plant source of essential fatty acids, notably linoeic acid (an omega 6) and alpha-linelenic acid (an omega 3). Rapeseed oil also contains both vitamins E and K. It can be used as an ingredient and for frying.

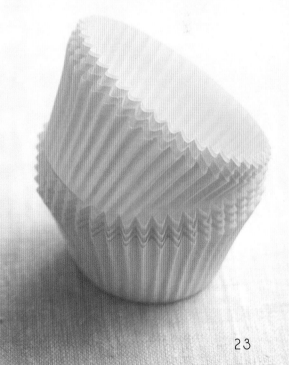

Irish soda bread has long been a personal favourite. There is no yeast or rising time to contend with, so if breadmaking seems time consuming or daunting, don't think of this as a bread; it is as easy as cake! Because this comes together so quickly, it can be made fresh on the day and is ideal for weekend breakfasts. It is always best on the day it was made, though it is still good, toasted, a few days later. The combination of bread, cream cheese and fruit spread tastes wickedly reminiscent of cheesecake but, here, the addition of oats to the loaf makes it more substantial and virtuous so go on and indulge.

Irish soda bread with fruit spread

250 g/2 cups plain/
    all-purpose flour
250 g/2 cups wholemeal/
    whole-wheat flour
100 g/1¾ cups porridge
    oats
1 teaspoon bicarbonate
    of soda/baking soda
1 teaspoon fine sea salt
30 g/2 tablespoons butter
400 ml/1⅓ cups buttermilk
1 tablespoon honey
cream cheese, to serve

FRUIT SPREAD
1 apple, peeled and
    finely chopped
400 g/2 cups fresh or frozen
    fruit of your choice, such
    as apricots, strawberries
    or mixed red berries
200 g/1 cup sugar

MAKES ABOUT 250 ML/1 CUP

Preheat the oven to 200°C (400°F) Gas 6.

Put the flours, oats, bicarbonate of soda/baking soda and salt in a mixing bowl and stir well. Add the butter and work in with your fingertips.

Combine the buttermilk and honey in a measuring jug/pitcher and stir to blend.

Make a well in the middle of the flour mixture and pour in the buttermilk. Stir to obtain a soft dough. You may need to add a bit more milk; the softer the dough the softer the bread so don't hesitate if it seems heavy, but add gradually.

Transfer to a lightly floured surface and knead gently for 2–3 minutes, until the dough is smooth and soft. Shape into a round, dust the top lightly with flour and make a large x-shaped slash in the top with a sharp knife.

Transfer to a baking sheet and bake in the preheated oven for 50–55 minutes, until the bread sounds hollow when the bottom is tapped. Let cool on a wire rack.

To make the fruit spread, put the apple and prepared fruit in a large saucepan (if using stone fruit, remove the pits and chop finely). Simmer, uncovered, for about 15 minutes, until tender. Stir in the sugar and simmer for a further 3–5 minutes, until the sugar has dissolved.

Transfer to a food processor and process until smooth. At this point, you can transfer the mixture to a jar for a fresher, thinner consistency, or return it to the pan and continue simmering for about 15 minutes more, until reduced and very thick, for a more intense spread. Although this is not a proper preserve due to the low sugar content, I always store in sterilized jars, to be sure. The spread will keep for up to 7–10 days if stored in a sterlized, sealed jar in the fridge.

To serve, slice the cooled soda bread thickly spread with cream cheese and serve the fruit spread alongside.

I wanted to devise a recipe that mimics commercial cereal bars, because they are such a good way to get breakfast food in on busy mornings but they are not always as healthy as they claim. This works well and is based on English flapjacks, which usually contain only oats alongside lashings of butter. The wheat-free mix gets in a range of different grains, seeds and fruit as stealthily as possible. It has a high success rate; one apple-hater I know eats these with gusto. If you want to dress this up for a special occasion, such as a party or a cake sale, throw in some dark chocolate chips or drizzle over some melted chocolate after slicing. Ideal for lunchboxes or after school snacks as well.

multigrain granola bars

125 g/1 stick butter

2 tablespoons honey

1 apple, unpeeled (if organic) and grated

1 generous tablespoon golden/light corn syrup

150 g/1½ cups porridge oats

100 g/1 cup barley flakes

50 g/½ cup millet or quinoa flakes

50 g/⅔ cup dessicated coconut (unsweetened)

4 tablespoons linseeds

3 tablespoons ground almonds or sunflower seeds (optional)

a large handful of raisins

a pinch of fine sea salt

100 ml/⅓ cup rapeseed oil

a 20 x 30-cm/8 x 12-inch non-stick baking sheet, lightly greased

MAKES 12–15 BARS

Preheat the oven to 180ºC (350ºF) Gas 4.

Put the butter and honey in a small saucepan and warm over low heat until just melted. Stir in the grated apple and syrup and set aside.

Combine the oats, barley flakes, millet, coconut, linseeds, almonds, raisins and salt in a large bowl and toss to combine.

Mix the melted butter mixture with the oil and stir into the dry ingredients with a wooden spoon until combined. Transfer to the prepared baking sheet and spread evenly.

Bake in the preheated oven for 10–12 minutes, until just golden around the edges for slightly chewy bars, or longer if crunchy bars are desired. Let cool slightly on the baking sheet, then cut into bars and transfer to a wire rack to cool completely. These bars will keep for 7–10 days if stored in an airtight container in the fridge.

Variation For Nutty Granola Bars add 4–5 tablespoons nut butter such as hazelnut or peanut (chunky or smooth) to the butter mixture (see page 36).

homemade granola

300 g/3 cups porridge oats
150 g/1½ cups barley flakes
50 g/½ cup millet or quinoa
flakes
90 g/1 cup flaked almonds
70 g/½ cup hulled sunflower
seeds
6 tablespoon linseeds

100 g/1 cup dessicated coconut
140 g/1 cup raisins, or any dried
fruit, chopped if necessary
125–250 ml/½–1 cup honey
2 tablespoons vegetable oil
fine sea salt

MAKES ABOUT 8–10 SERVINGS

Preheat the oven to 170ºC (325ºF) Gas 3.

Combine all the dry ingredients, except the raisins, in a large mixing bowl. Add a pinch of salt and toss to mix.

If the honey is thick, soften slightly by heating gently over low heat or in a microwave. Stir together the honey and oil, then pour into the oat mixture and mix well.

Spread the oat mixture in an even layer on a large baking sheet. Bake in the preheated oven for 10 minutes then stir. Continue baking for 10–20 minutes more, stirring once or twice, until golden. Stir in the raisins and let cool on the baking sheet. When cool, transfer to an airtight container and store at room temperature in a cool dark place. Use within 1 week.

cereal bar

Think of this as a breakfast salad bar. The idea is to get kids varying their nutritional intake which, put that way, sounds dull and unappetizing. This is not practical for weekdays, it is definitely a special occasion breakfast, ideal after a sleepover or when on holiday – perhaps in a large group. A benefit of serving breakfast this way is it may prompt children to try cereals they have never tried before, which is important and often difficult. Well-stocked health food shops offer a range of grain and cereal flakes and puffs, which can be used here in addition to supermarket boxed brands. Simply arrange all the components on the table, offer bowls and let everyone help themselves. There are a few less than nutritionally sound offerings, intended to maintain the festive spirit and to be used sparingly. You need not offer everything on the list; the selection can be as big or small as you like. All the dry ingredients keep well but if there is any fresh fruit leftover, why not make some smoothies (see page 20)?.

A selection of cereals
Puffed rice
Quinoa puffs
Spelt flakes
Wheat hoops
Puffed corn
Corn flakes
Malted wheat squares
Muesli
Homemade granola (see left)

Dessicated coconut
Small dried fruit, preferably
    unsweetened, such as
    blueberries, cherries or
    cranberries
Chopped dried fruit, such as
    apples, peaches or apricots
Dark chocolate chips
Cinnamon sugar
Sugar sprinkles

Dry toppings
Chopped nuts (pistachios,
    pecans, macadamias,
    cashews and/or Brazils)
Ground nuts (almonds and/
    or hazelnuts)
Seeds (linseed, sunflower
    and/or sesame)
Raisins or sultanas/golden
    raisins

Wet toppings
Slices of fresh or canned fruit
    (unsweetened in juice)
Fruit coulis
Yogurt, plain or flavoured
Milk or non-dairy milk
    alternatives, such as soya,
    rice or almond milks
Honey, maple syrup or
    agave nectar

This is ideal for using up a stale loaf. Any dried fruit can be used, alone or in combination, as can different breads. Fresh fruit is also nice; diced apple is ideal (as is pear), pitted cherries, strawberries and even rhubarb, if you can convince your children to try some, though you may need to increase the sugar quantity.

breakfast bread & butter pudding with dried apricots & cranberries

**about 500 ml/2 cups milk
(you may need a little
more if your bread is
thickly sliced)**

2 tablespoons sugar

3 eggs

**¼ teaspoon ground
cinnamon**

**8 slices wholemeal bread,
torn into bite-size pieces**

**170 g/1 cup dried apricots,
chopped**

**4 tablespoons dried
cranberries
(unsweetened)**

**honey or maple syrup,
for drizzling**

a baking dish, generously
greased with butter

SERVES 4–6 CHILDREN

Preheat the oven to 180°C (350°F) Gas 4.

Combine the milk, sugar, eggs and cinnamon in a bowl and whisk well to blend. Set aside.

Put the apricot pieces and cranberries in a small bowl and mix well.

Arrange half of the bread pieces in the prepared baking dish and sprinkle with half of the apricot mixture. Top with the remaining bread and the remaining apricot mixture and pour over the milk mixture.

Bake in the preheated oven for about 35–45 minutes, until puffed, golden and just slightly wobbly in the middle.

Serve warm, with honey or maple syrup to drizzle over.

Porridge is not something I often make for more than one at a time, so this is a recipe for a single serving. The idea is that it takes one measure of oats to one and a half measures of milk, so it is very easy to increase this as needed without resorting to scales or measuring jugs – simply grab a glass. The banana and almond enhance the flavour beautifully as well as adding nutrition. The same is true for the ground sunflower seeds, which are so healthful yet so difficult to get into a child's diet.

banana & almond porridge

1 glass porridge oats
1½ glasses milk
**1 small ripe banana,
    mashed**
**1–2 tablespoons ground
    almonds**
**1–2 tablespoons ground
    sunflower seeds
    (optional)**
**a good pinch of ground
    cinnamon (optional)**

TO SERVE
**honey or dark soft
    brown sugar**
chilled milk

MAKES 1 SERVING

For the stovetop method, put the oats and milk in a saucepan and bring to the boil. Lower the heat and simmer, stirring often, for 2–3 minutes. Add the banana and almonds and simmer for 1–2 minutes more, stirring often. Stir in the sunflower seeds if using.

For the microwave method, combine the oats and milk in a glass bowl and microwave on high for 1½ minutes. Remove, stir in the banana and almonds and microwave for 1 minute more. Stir in the sunflower seeds if using.

Transfer to a serving bowl, sprinkle with the cinnamon (if using), and top with a spoonful or so of honey or sugar (or one of each!). Serve immediately, with extra milk to thin and cool.

Variation Sweeten with 2–3 tablespoons Fruit Spread (see page 24) instead of honey and/or sugar.

Note Ground sunflower seeds are difficult to find. I make my own by grinding the hulled seeds in a coffee grinder. The seeds are so small this is the only machine which works. I rarely use more than a few tablespoons at a time, but I make as big a batch as I can and then keep in an airtight container in the fridge for several weeks.

OATS
Although oats are primarily a carbohydrate, compared to other grains, they also contain relatively high levels of protein. They are also a useful plant source of thiamin, riboflavin and B6, as well as minerals: calcium, magnesium, iron and zinc. Oats are also a low-GI food, useful for providing a steady release of energy and helping us to feel fuller for longer, thus they are the ideal breakfast food for busy children.

This is an everything-but-the-kitchen-sink recipe and one that is difficult to make the same way twice. The idea is to use it as a means to both feed the family a good breakfast and clear the vegetable rack of inconveniently small quantities of vegetables. If there is a small piece of cheese lurking, grate that into the eggs as well. The recipe calls for bits and pieces but, really, use this as a springboard rather than gospel and see if you too can start the day by clearing the fridge. For some reason, the unpredictability ensures this is always delicious.

scrambled egg surprise

6 large eggs
2–3 tablespoons milk
3 tablespoons cottage
   cheese (optional)
1 small onion, finely
   chopped or grated
½ red, yellow or green
   (bell) pepper, diced
a few mushrooms, diced
1 celery stick, diced
1 cooked potato, diced
1 cooked vegetarian
   sausage, diced
a few cherry tomatoes,
   quartered
unsalted butter and
   vegetable oil, for cooking
sea salt and black pepper

TO SERVE
wholemeal/whole-wheat
   toast
Tabasco, tomato ketchup
   or brown sauce

MAKES 4 SERVINGS

Combine the eggs, milk and cottage cheese (if using) in a bowl and whisk to blend well. Season lightly with salt and pepper and set aside.

Heat about 1 tablespoon oil and a knob of butter in a non-stick frying pan/skillet. Add the onion, pepper, mushrooms and celery and cook, stirring often, for 3–5 minutes, until soft. Season lightly. Add the potato, sausage and tomatoes and cook for 1–2 minutes, to warm through.

Pour in the egg mixture and cook, stirring with a wooden spatula, until the eggs begin to set.

Divide the mixture between serving plates and serve immediately with plenty of toast and your preferred bottled sauce.

Mushrooms and cream is an irresistible combination but if this seems a bit too rich for a morning meal, plain sautéed mushrooms are just as good. A few thickly sliced tomatoes, quickly seared in some oil in a pan, make a nice accompaniment, as does a poached egg or two.

mushrooms on toast

500 g/1 lb. mushrooms, wiped and quartered or sliced
1 tablespoon unsalted butter
2–3 tablespoons vegetable oil
1 garlic clove, crushed (optional)
chopped fresh flat-leaf parsley

150 ml/²⁄₃ cup single/light cream
4 slices wholemeal/ whole-wheat toast
sea salt and black pepper

MAKES 2 SERVINGS

Heat the butter and oil in a non-stick frying pan/skillet. Add the mushrooms and cook for about 10 minutes, stirring occasionally, until tender and golden. Season to taste.

Stir in the garlic (if using) and parsley and cook for about 1 minute, then add the cream and simmer gently for 2–3 minutes. Taste and adjust the seasoning.

Serve immediately on the toast.

Nut butters are a fantastic way to get nutrients into a vegetarian child's diet. However many commercial preparations, especially peanut butters, contain unhealthy hydrogenated fats as well as high levels of fructose corn syrup. A better option is to make your own, though children who are accustomed to commercial butters may not enjoy the taste and texture of homemade at first, hence the addition of honey which is intended to make this recipe more appealing. To involve the children in the preparation, use nuts in their shells and put them to work shelling. There is no need to remove any skins.

nut butters

165 g/1 cup whole shelled nuts, such as almonds, cashews, peanuts or hazelnuts
a pinch of fine sea salt

1 tablespoon vegetable oil
1 tablespoon honey or agave nectar (optional)

MAKES ABOUT 250 ML/1 CUP

Preheat the oven to 175ºC (350ºF) Gas 4.

Spread the nuts out in a single layer on a baking sheet and roast in the preheated oven for about 10–20 minutes, until golden and aromatic – they should be just toasted. If using dark skinned nuts, such as almonds, use your nose as a guide and do not roast longer than 20 minutes to be certain.

Transfer the nuts to a food processor fitted with a chopping blade and add the salt. Begin processing to obtain a paste. Blend in the oil if necessary to thin the mixture, and the honey (if using). The butter will keep for up to 2 weeks if stored in a jar in the fridge.

Note This butter will separate more than commercial butters, which is normal. To make it easier to stir before serving, store in a jar that is slightly larger than the volume.

lunchboxes
& snacks

Wraps look nice and make a pleasant change from ordinary sandwiches. Flour tortillas make the best wrapper but large supermarkets often stock other types of flatbreads made especially for wraps as these have become popular. If wholemeal/whole-wheat tortillas are available, they are the best choice. This is a fairly sophisticated filling which may not appeal to all ages; for something much simpler, try a basic combination of cream cheese and avocado slices.

avocado & chickpea wrap

4 wholemeal/whole-wheat tortillas or other wraps

410-g/14-oz. can chickpeas drained and rinsed

4 generous spoonfuls cottage cheese

1 ripe avocado, thinly sliced

1 tomato, deseeded and flesh diced

3–4 tablespoons grated vegetarian cheddar

a few handfuls of shredded little gem lettuce and/or sprouted seeds

a little freshly squeezed lemon juice

rapeseed oil or extra virgin olive oil, for drizzling

sea salt and black pepper

MAKES 2–4 SERVINGS

Working one at a time, put a tortilla on the work surface. Sprinkle one fourth of the chickpeas on top, in a line down the middle. Mash lightly with a fork, spreading out in a half-moon shape towards one edge of the tortilla.

Cover this with a generous spoonful of cottage cheese. Arrange a few avocado slices on top, in a line down the middle.

Sprinkle over a small handful of diced tomato, a little grated cheddar and some lettuce.

Squeeze over a little lemon juice, season lightly and finish with a drizzle of oil.

Starting from the edge with the filling, begin rolling to enclose the filling. Cut in half and serve immediately, with the seam-side down.

Other filling ideas for wraps

Cream Cheese and Barley spread Make a spread using 200 g/1 cup cream cheese mixed with 200 g/1 cup cooked barley. Season with a pinch of celery salt and a pinch of garlic granules. Spread this on a wrap and top with thin strips of celery, red (bell) pepper, shredded lettuce and grated carrot. Sprinkle with finely grated cheese, add a squeeze of fresh lemon juice and roll up.

Tofu salad Mash some firm tofu in a bowl with a few spoonfuls of mayonnaise. Stir in some finely chopped celery, thinly sliced spring onions/scallions, finely grated cheese and a pinch of dry mustard powder. Season lightly with salt and pepper. Spread on a wrap, top with sprouted seeds or shredded lettuce and roll up.

Egg, cheese and tomato Spread some freshly prepared scrambled eggs or egg mayonnaise over a wrap, sprinkle with some finely grated cheese and diced tomatoes and roll up.

super-nutritious sandwiches

Use wholemeal/whole-wheat slices, rolls or bagels and organic whenever possible. This is particularly important for children, as pesticide levels may be higher in unrefined grains. If your children like seeded bread, even better. Some like German-style rye breads – these are usually full of seeds and wheat-free. Use any of the combinations given as is, or spread the bread lightly with butter. Alternative spreads include organic yeast pastes, salad dressings, a light drizzle of olive oil and/or balsamic vinegar (over the filling rather than on the bread otherwise it gets too soggy) or a pesto sauce (see page 83).

To 'sneak in' some extra nutrients, any of the combinations here can be sprinkled with finely ground sunflower seeds, or a mix of ground sunflower and pumpkin seeds, and perhaps a sprinkling of linseeds. To obtain the ground mixture, it's best to use a coffee grinder. Grind in small batches and these will keep in a sealed container in the fridge for at least 4–5 days. Some health food shops offer ground seed mixes, which is convenient but pricey. Nut and seed butters also make a nutritious filling (see page 36) and a wide range is available in larger supermarkets and health food stores. However, due to allergy issues, nut products can be problematic so do check the rules about nuts in school (or other group settings) before sending your child off with a nut butter sandwich.

Avoid packing sandwiches in disposable wrappers to keep waste to a minimum. Small plastic or stainless steel, lidded containers can be reused. There is some controversy as to 'safe' plastics for food use so containers which are BPA- and phthalate-free are recommended.

Basic sandwich filling ideas

Cream cheese

+ topped with finely chopped celery and sultanas/golden raisins

+ grated apple or carrot with or without chopped olives

+ finely chopped dried fruit, such as apricots or prunes

+ deseeded cucumber slices, with or without chopped olives

Cottage cheese

+ sliced or mashed avocado with a drizzle of balsamic vinegar

+ sprouted seeds and chopped tomatoes with or without olives

+ finely chopped canned pineapple or peaches (drained)

+ cooked butternut squash or pumpkin, slightly mashed

Vegetarian cheddar cheese

+ sliced cheese with tomato slices, shredded lettuce, sliced pickles and 1000 Island dressing

+ grated cheese topped with drained and mashed baked beans or kidney beans

+ grated cheese with homemade Coleslaw (see page 46)

+ grated cheese mixed with diced tomatoes, mayonnaise and shredded lettuce or fresh spinach

Ricotta

+ mixed with some Vegetable Bolognese (see page 125)

+ chopped cooked spinach with homemade Pesto (see page 83)

+ sweetcorn and/or chopped olives and finely grated cheese

Houmous (see page 44)

+ finely grated carrots

+ seeded, cored and thinly sliced red (bell) pepper

+ shredded lettuce or fresh spinach with a drizzle of balsamic vinegar

+ pine kernels or sesame seeds

Other ideas

Potato and Sweet Potato Squares (see page 52), thinly sliced with mayonnaise

Chickpea Bites (see page 51) with mayonnaise and shredded lettuce

Bean and Tofu Dip (see page 44) with grated carrots, sprouted seeds or shredded lettuce

Nut butter (see page 36) or seed butter with chopped dried fruit, such as apricots

Peanut butter with honey and grated carrot or mashed banana

Mashed avocado and diced tomato with chopped black olives

It is useful to have a selection of healthy dips on hand for packing into lunches, offering as snacks or serving as jacket potato fillings. Commercially made dips are a good shortcut, but here is a selection of easy to make recipes, tasty and wholesome and, most importantly, homemade, thereby reducing the amount of processed foods in your child's diet.

houmous

410-g/14-oz. can chickpeas, drained and rinsed
2 tablespoons tahini (sesame seed paste), or more to taste
3 tablespoons extra virgin olive oil or rapeseed oil, or a combination of both

½ teaspoon fine sea salt
freshly squeezed juice of ½ a lemon
1–2 tablespoons apple juice (optional)

MAKES ABOUT 450 G/2 CUPS

Put all the ingredients in the bowl of a food processor and process to obtain a smooth paste. If the mixture is too thick add water, 1 tablespoon at a time, to obtain the desired consistency. Taste and adjust the seasoning; use apple juice to make it sweeter if liked. The houmous will keep for 2–3 days if stored in an airtight container in the fridge.

Variations A variety of ingredients can be stirred into houmous to boost the flavour and widen the range of nutrients. The possibilities are endless so do experiment, but here are some ideas: 2–3 chopped oven-roasted plum tomatoes; a large handful of chopped red peppers from a jar; a large handful of chopped pitted olives; a few pieces of cooked butternut squash or sweet potato, finely diced; 1–2 tablespoons ground sunflower seeds; a large handful of pine kernels, grated carrot and/or beetroot; or a mixture of chopped fresh herbs such as flat-leaf parsley, chives or basil. Adding fresh ingredients may shorten the fridge life so if unsure, taste a small amount and/or use your nose.

bean & tofu dip

410-g/14-oz. can mixed beans, drained
4–7 tablespoons silken tofu

1 tablespoon balsamic vinegar
sea salt and black pepper

MAKES ABOUT 500 ML/2 CUPS

Put the beans and 4 tablespoon tofu in the bowl of a food processor and process until smooth. Add more tofu as desired for a thinner texture. Transfer to a bowl, stir in the vinegar and season to taste. Serve with crudités.

The dip will keep for 2–3 days if stored in an airtight container in the fridge.

charlie's tomato jam

1 small onion, finely chopped
2–4 tablespoons vegetable oil
325 g/12 oz. cherry tomatoes
1 garlic clove, crushed
a pinch of dried red chilli/hot pepper flakes (or 1 fresh green chilli, seeded and finely chopped)
a large pinch of sugar

a large handful of fresh flat-leaf parsley or coriander/ cilantro leaves, chopped (optional)
1 tablespoon freshly squeezed lemon juice or balsamic vinegar (optional)
sea salt and black pepper

MAKES ABOUT 450 G/2 CUPS

Put the onion and oil in a medium frying pan/skillet and cook over low heat until soft.

Add the tomatoes, garlic, chilli and sugar and season lightly. Stir well, then cover with a lid and simmer gently for about 10 minutes, stirring occasionally with a wooden spoon, until the tomatoes burst. If dry, add a little bit more oil.

Taste and adjust the seasoning. Stir in the herbs and lemon juice or balsamic vinegar, if using.

This is a slightly grown up salad, and the recipe is conventional, but it contains many ingredients children enjoy. If your children only like some but not all of these, please adjust as required. Even the basic combo of couscous and raisins (perhaps increase the amount of raisins) makes a delicious salad and is very nutritious as well. Ideas for less conventional additions are included in the variations, below. The taste will improve on standing so this is ideal for making ahead to fill lunchboxes all week long or simply to have on hand as a snack.

couscous salad

225 g/1 cup wholemeal/ whole–wheat couscous
410-g/14-oz. can chickpeas, drained and rinsed
75 g/½ cup raisins
½ tablespoon chopped fresh flat-leaf parsley leaves
½ red (bell) pepper, diced

a handful of pine kernels
freshly squeezed juice of ½–1 lemon
4–7 tablespoons extra virgin olive oil
sea salt and black pepper

MAKES 6–8 SMALL SERVINGS

Cook the couscous according to package instructions. When cool, transfer to a large bowl. Add the chickpeas, raisins, parsley, red pepper and pine kernels. Squeeze in the juice of ½ a lemon and add 4 tablespoons of the oil. Season lightly and toss to blend. Taste, adding more lemon juice and oil as desired.

Variations Ingredients which can be finely diced and added in addition to, or to replace any in the basic recipe, include: celery, seeded cherry tomatoes, shallots, fennel, cooked butternut squash, pumpkin or sweet potato, clementine or orange segments and halved seedless grapes.

A very quick, basic recipe for a family favourite, this is ideal as part of a simple meal any day of the week. Any type of pasta can be used, including ordinary white pasta, or use a mix of half white and half wholemeal. Do try to choose a small shape which will allow the vegetables to nestle inside the pasta.

pasta salad

200 g/2 cups pasta shapes
140 g/1 cup edamame or baby lima beans, briefly boiled
165 g/1 cup cooked sweetcorn kernels (canned or frozen)
2 carrots, grated
4–6 tablespoons mayonnaise
freshly squeezed juice of ½ a lemon

a handful of fresh flat-leaf parsley leaves, chopped (optional)
sea salt and black pepper

MAKES 6–8 SMALL SERVINGS

Cook the pasta according to the package instructions. When cool, transfer to a bowl and add the edamame, sweetcorn, carrots and mayonnaise and mix well. Add the lemon juice and parsley and season to taste. Mix, taste and adjust the seasoning. Cover and refrigerate until ready to serve.

Variation For Pesto Pasta Salad, dress the cooked pasta with 2 tablespoons mayonnaise and 2 tablespoons pesto sauce of your choice (see page 83). Add more mayonnaise and/or pesto as desired.

You can slice the cabbage by hand but I found that, since I got the food processor out to do the carrots, it was just as easy to carry on using the grater attachment. This results in a different texture from most commercial coleslaws but it is actually easier to eat when grated, especially for little teeth, and it makes a less messy sandwich filling this way as well. The mix of white and red cabbage boosts the nutrients and gives it a vibrant pink colour, but all white cabbage can also be used for a more conventional mixture. The apple adds sweetness thus replacing the sugar called for in many recipes. If desired, add some ground sunflower seeds to individual portions just before serving.

coleslaw

200 g/7 oz. red cabbage, cored
375 g/13 oz. white cabbage, cored
200 g/7 oz. carrots, unpeeled if organic
1 small apple, peeled
about 100 g/⅓ cup mayonnaise
freshly squeezed juice of ½ a lemon

½ teaspoon fine sea salt
a large handful of sultanas/ golden raisins (optional)
ground sunflower seeds (optional)

MAKES 8–10 SMALL SERVINGS

Using a food processor fitted with a grater attachment, grate the red and white cabbage, carrots and apple.

Transfer the grated vegetables and apple to a large bowl. Add the mayonnaise, lemon juice and salt and stir well to combine. Stir in the sultanas/golden raisins (if using). Taste and adjust the seasoning, adding more salt, lemon juice and mayonnaise as required. Cover and refrigerate until ready to serve.

This salad was a staple of deli counter offerings when I was a child and in those days, it was usually made with green beans from a can, which are soggy and come in an unappetizing shade of khaki. I've updated the recipe using fresh beans for an improved taste and appearance. Cooked quinoa, a cupful or so, makes a tasty and nutritious addition.

three-bean salad

200 g/7 oz. green beans
410-g/14-oz. can chickpeas, drained and rinsed
410-g/14-oz. can kidney beans, drained and rinsed
2–3 spring onions/scallions, finely chopped
a large handful of chopped fresh flat-leaf parsley leaves (optional)

FOR THE DRESSING
1 teaspoon Dijon mustard
1 tablespoon red wine vinegar
5 tablespoons extra virgin olive oil
sea salt and black pepper

MAKES 6–8 SMALL SERVINGS

To make the dressing, put the mustard, vinegar and a good pinch of salt in a large bowl and whisk together. Gradually add the oil, 1 tablespoon at a time until thick and blended. If a tangy dressing is desired, add another teaspoon or so of vinegar. Set aside.

Bring a saucepan of water to the boil. Trim the green beans, add to the pan and cook for about 5 minutes, until just tender. Drain and refresh under cold running water. Pat dry with paper towels and slice into ½-cm/¼-inch pieces. Put the green beans, chickpeas and kidney beans in the bowl with the dressing and toss well. Taste and adjust the seasoning. Add the spring onions/scallions and parsley (if using). Cover and refrigerate until ready to serve.

Variation Not everyone likes kidney beans (it's something to do with the texture) so these can be replaced with some diced, seeded cucumber, a diced green or red (bell) pepper, or a small punnet of seeded and chopped cherry tomatoes.

These nifty bite-size morsels are quick to prepare, and you can enlist young kitchen helpers to aid with the ball shaping. They are very good dipped in Greek yogurt but no lives will be lost if ketchup is what makes them go down. These reheat well so it's worth making a large batch to enjoy over a few days or for the freezer (defrost before reheating). Serve with brown rice and sliced raw vegetables: cucumbers, cherry tomatoes, carrots and celery. They are also good cold as a sandwich filler, with mayonnaise and some shredded lettuce.

chickpea bites

1 small onion, coarsely chopped

1 carrot, coarsely chopped

1 celery stick, coarsely chopped

1 garlic clove, peeled

2–3 tablespoons extra virgin olive oil or rapeseed oil

410-g/14-oz. tin chickpeas, drained and rinsed

2 generous tablespoons mayonnaise

2 tablespoons oatbran

1 tablespoon wholemeal/ whole-wheat flour

freshly squeezed juice of ½ an orange

sea salt and black pepper

plain Greek yogurt, to serve (optional)

a non-stick baking sheet, lightly greased

MAKES 12–15 BITES

Preheat the oven to 200ºC (400ºF) Gas 6.

Put the onion, carrot, celery and garlic in the bowl of a food processor and process until finely chopped.

Heat the oil in a small non-stick frying pan/skillet. When hot, add the vegetable mixture, season with salt and pepper and cook for 3–5 minutes, stirring often until soft. Do not allow the mixture to brown or the garlic will taste bitter. Let cool slightly.

Meanwhile, put the chickpeas, mayonnaise, oatbran, flour and orange juice into the same food processor bowl and process, leaving some small chunks of chickpea; it should not be completely smooth. Transfer the chickpea mixture to a large bowl. Add the vegetable mixture and stir well. Taste and adjust the seasoning.

Form the mixture into walnut-size balls and arrange on the prepared baking sheet. Bake in the preheated oven for 30–40 minutes, until brown and just golden on top. Serve, hot, warm or at room temperature.

Variation For adults or children with more sophisticated palates, replace the orange juice with lemon juice and add a large handful of chopped fresh herbs, such as coriander/cilantro and/or flat-leaf parsley and a finely chopped small red chilli to the mixture just before shaping into balls. For a grown up dipping sauce, stir some chopped fresh mint, crushed garlic and grated cucumber into the yogurt.

This is a baked Spanish-style tortilla, but with sweet peppers and some cheese added for extra flavour and goodness. Great served hot with a salad for lunch or dinner or cold in lunchboxes. It's equally good sliced thinly and used as a sandwich filling with a little mayonnaise.

potato & sweet pepper squares

450 g/1 lb. waxy potatoes

2–3 tablespoons extra
   virgin olive oil

1 onion, halved and sliced

1 red (bell) pepper, halved,
   deseeded and sliced

6 eggs

4 tablespoons milk

a large handful of chopped
   fresh flat-leaf parsley or
   snipped chives (optional)

100 g/1 cup grated
   vegetarian cheddar

sea salt and black pepper

a 25-cm/10-inch square
non-stick cake tin/pan,
generously greased

MAKES 12 SQUARES

Peel the potatoes and put them in a large saucepan with enough cold water to cover. Simmer until just tender and drain. When cool enough to handle, slice thinly. Set aside.

Preheat the oven to 200ºC (400ºF) Gas 6.

Heat the oil in a frying pan/skillet and add the onion and pepper. Cook for 3–5 minutes, until just soft. Season lightly.

Whisk the eggs and milk together in a bowl and add the chopped herbs (if using). Season with 1 teaspoon salt and a generous grinding of pepper.

Arrange the onion mixture in the bottom of the prepared tin/pan. Top with the potato slices and sprinkle over the grated cheddar. Pour in the egg mixture, tilting the pan to coat evenly.

Bake in the preheated oven for 20–25 minutes, until puffed and just set. Cut into squares and serve hot, warm or at room temperature. The squares will keep for 2–3 days if stored in an airtight container in the fridge.

Cooking for children should not require complex preparations in order to provide a healthy and delicious meal. Sometimes it is just the ideas that are lacking. So this is an idea recipe; other types of bread can be used in place of the pitta – wholemeal/whole-wheat bagels and baguettes are especially good. If you can persuade your children to eat them, the ends of a sliced wholemeal loaf make a very good pizza base. There are many good quality tomato sauces available, look for those that are low in salt and sugar. If you want to involve the kids in the meal preparation, this is a good place to start. With a bit of supervision, they can assemble the pizzas themselves and choose their own toppings.

easy–peasy pitta pizzas

4 wholemeal/whole-wheat pitta breads or similar (see recipe introduction for other suggestions)
350-g/12-oz. jar ready-made pizza or pasta sauce, any flavour
200 g/2 cups grated vegetarian cheddar or firm mozzarella

SUGGESTED TOPPINGS
sweetcorn
pitted, sliced black olives
diced (bell) peppers
vegetarian sausage slices
sliced mushrooms
sliced tomatoes
grated onion
grated courgette/zucchini
grated butternut squash
baked beans

MAKES 4 PIZZAS

Preheat the grill/broiler and line the pan with foil to catch any drips.

Put the pitta breads on a work surface. Spread each one with a good layer of sauce and sprinkle over some grated cheese.

Arrange the toppings of your choice on top of the cheese. Cook the pitta pizzas under the preheated grill/broiler for 4–5 minutes, until just bubbling.

Serve immediately, taking care as the melted cheese will be very hot.

These make a great afterschool snack, or a nice addition to a lunchbox as a replacement for a sandwich; as is, or split and spread with some cream cheese. They also make a good breakfast option when eating on the run. The intention, however, is to make this to serve alongside one of the quick and easy soups on pages 64–71. This is a very good recipe to prepare with children and making a large loaf, rather than individual scones, certainly speeds things up but feel free to make individual scones if preferred.

cheese & sunflower seed scones

125 g/1 cup plain/
  all-purpose flour
125 g/1 cup wholemeal/
  whole-wheat flour
¼ teaspoon fine sea salt
1 generous teaspoon
  baking powder
75 g/5 tablespoons
  unsalted butter,
  at room temperature
  and cut into pieces
2 tablespoons sunflower
  seeds
65 g/½ cup grated
  vegetarian cheddar
150 ml/⅔ cup milk

a non-stick baking sheet,
lightly greased

MAKES 8 SCONES

Preheat the oven to 180°C (350°F) Gas 4.

Put both the flours, salt and baking powder in a mixing bowl. Add the butter and work in with your fingertips, rubbing to obtain coarse crumbs.

Add the milk and stir to obtain a soft dough (which, if you are accustomed to making plain/all-purpose flour only mixtures, will be slightly heavier). Stir in the grated cheddar and sunflower seeds.

Transfer the dough to a lightly floured surface and use a rolling pin to roll out to a loaf about 4 cm/1½ inches thick. Using a large, sharp knife, cut into eighths, slicing almost but not all the way through; you're just scoring portion marks for later.

Carefully transfer the loaf to the prepared baking sheet and bake in the preheated oven for 25–35 minutes, until just browned and risen. Serve warm or at room temperature. The scones will keep for 2–3 days if stored in an airtight container.

Variation For adults or children with sophisticated palates, replace the cheddar with crumbled blue cheese, and the sunflower seeds with 3 tablespoons chopped walnuts. Alternatively, use crumbled feta in place of the cheddar and chopped sun-dried tomatoes or black olives in place of the seeds.

This recipe will be familiar to Americans as it is pretty much a staple item, with good reason as this is quick to make and ideal any time of day. It is much like cake in texture, and can even be a bit on the sweet side if you add honey, which is how many children like it. Cornbread makes a nice lunchbox item, but is equally useful as an after-school snack, an accompaniment to soups and casseroles at the dinner table, and is tasty spread with butter at breakfast. Squares are the easiest way to make this, though you could also make muffins with the same recipe, and some speciality shops stock traditional cornbread (corn pone) pans, which make individual breads shaped like a cob of corn.

cornbread

175 g/1 cup cornmeal

**150 g/1 cup plain/
all-purpose flour**

2 teaspoons baking powder

¼ teaspoon fine sea salt

1 egg, beaten

**250 ml/1 cup plain yogurt
or buttermilk, plus extra
milk if required**

**2 tablespoons honey
(optional)**

**3 tablespoons vegetable oil
or melted unsalted butter**

a 18-cm/7-inch square baking tin/pan, generously buttered

MAKES 12–16 SQUARES

Preheat the oven to 190ºC (375ºF) Gas 5.

Put the cornmeal, flour, baking powder and salt in a mixing bowl and mix well.

Put the egg, yogurt, honey (if using) and oil or melted butter in a separate bowl or measuring jug/pitcher and mix well. Pour this into the cornmeal mixture and stir in. If the batter is heavy, gradually add some extra milk to thin. If the batter is too heavy, the cornbread will be dry, so add enough milk to obtain a soft mixture; not as thin as a cake batter, but certainly not as stiff as a bread dough.

Spoon the mixture into the prepared baking tin/pan and bake in the preheated oven for 25–35 minutes, until just golden around the edges and a knife inserted in the middle comes out clean. Let cool in the tin/pan for a few minutes before turning out to cool on a wire rack. Serve warm or at room temperature.

Variations Many things can be added to this basic recipe. Choose from sweetcorn, diced red and/or green (bell) peppers, chopped spring onions/scallions, grated or cubed cheese, pesto, herbs, nuts or seeds. It's best to omit the honey if you opt for any of the above additions.

This recipe uses a mix of flours and a low-sugar fruit spread, making it a healthier option for lunchboxes or after-school treats. The nuts also boost the nutritional value, as do the seeds. Any flavour fruit spread is suitable, or combine two different flavours to create something unique.

fruit & nut bars

160 g/1 cup wholemeal/ whole-wheat flour

230 g/1½ cups plain/ all-purpose flour

230 g/1 cup sugar

175 g/1½ sticks unsalted butter

a pinch of fine sea salt

2 x 280-g/10-oz. jars fruit spread (or see recipe on page 24)

110 g/1 cup mixed unsalted nuts, such as walnuts, pecans and hazelnuts

2–3 tablespoons linseeds or ground sunflower seeds

a 20–30-cm/8–12-inch baking sheet, lined with greaseproof paper and lightly oiled

MAKES 12–15 BARS

Preheat the oven to 180ºC (350ºF) Gas 4.

Put both the flours, sugar, butter and salt in the bowl of a food processor and pulse to obtain coarse crumbs. Alternatively, mix in a large bowl, using your fingertips to work the butter into the flour mixture, rubbing to obtain coarse crumbs.

Spread just over half of the mixture evenly over the prepared baking sheet, patting it down firmly. Spread the fruit spread on top in an even layer.

Add the nuts and seeds to the remaining flour mixture and stir to mix. Sprinkle loosely over the fruit spread layer to cover evenly.

Bake in the preheated oven for 25–35 minutes, until just brown around the edges. Let cool slightly on the baking sheet then slice into bars.

These bars will keep for 7–10 days if stored in an airtight container.

NUTS AND SEEDS

These should be an integral part of a vegetarian child's diet although due to allergy issues now being so prevalent, this is often difficult. If your child tolerates these ingredients be sure to include them as often as possible. They are a good source of protein, essential fats, calcium, magnesium and zinc. I keep a supply of ground seeds and nuts on hand ready to add to dishes.

soups
& fast food

There are two ways to serve this soup, it depends on the preferences of the young diners. They can choose from cheesy croûtons floating on the top or simply melted cheese on bread rounds for dipping.

Soup is a wholesome, easy way to feed children. This recipe is just a starting point – almost any vegetable can be used, singly or in combination and you can experiment with flavourings.

pizza soup

2–3 tablespoons rapeseed oil

500 g/1 lb. white onions, halved and thinly sliced

a handful of chopped flat-leaf parsley leaves (optional)

a splash of red wine (optional)

400-g/14-oz. can chopped tomatoes

1 tablespoon ketchup

a pinch of sugar

1 litre/4 cups vegetable stock

1 baguette, sliced into rounds

125-g/4½-oz. ball mozzarella, sliced

a pinch of dried oregano

pitted and sliced black olives, to serve (optional)

sea salt and black pepper

MAKES 6–8 SERVINGS

Heat the oil in a large saucepan and add the onions. Cook over low heat until soft. Stir in the parsley and wine (if using) and season lightly with salt and pepper. Cook until the liquid has evaporated. Stir in the tomatoes, ketchup, sugar and stock. Bring to the boil, then reduce the heat and simmer for at least 20 minutes. Taste and adjust the seasoning. The recipe can be made up to 24 hours in advance up to this point.

If 'bits' of onion and tomato will be rejected, purée the soup, either in a food processor or with a hand-held immersion blender.

To serve like onion soup, preheat the grill/broiler. Ladle the soup into heatproof serving bowls. Allow 2–3 bread slices per serving. Top each one with mozzarella, sprinkle lightly with oregano and a few olive slices (if using). Float the slices on top of the soup and run under the grill/broiler until browned and bubbling. Serve immediately, taking care as the bowls will be hot.

Alternatively, run the cheese-topped bread slices under the grill/broiler until browned and bubbling and serve alongside the soup for dipping.

Joseph's pureed carrot soup with lentils

1 tablespoon extra virgin olive oil or rapeseed oil

1 onion, finely chopped

3 carrots, finely diced

2–3 teaspoons mild curry powder

1 tablespoon grated fresh ginger (optional)

1½ litres/6 cups vegetable stock

100 g/½ cup red lentils, cooked and drained

sea salt and black pepper

MAKES 4–6 SERVINGS

Heat the oil in a large saucepan. Add the onion and carrots and cook for 3–5 minutes, until soft. Season lightly with salt and pepper. Add the curry powder and ginger (if using) and cook, stirring, for 1 minute. Add the stock and simmer for about 15 minutes, until tender. Stir in the lentils and cook to warm through. Purée the soup either in a food processor or with a hand-held immersion blender. Taste and adjust the seasoning. Serve immediately.

Variations Replace the lentils with haricot beans, chickpeas or diced cooked potato. You can also stir in a small can of chopped tomatoes. Use 1 carrot instead of 3 and add 1 large sweet potato; use 1 carrot and some finely chopped cauliflower. Stir in a handful of frozen peas after blending and cook until warmed through. Prepare the basic soup and omit the curry and ginger – flavour instead with a dollop of pesto (see page 83).

I had just received my weekly box of vegetables from the farm and this soup was simmering on the stove the day my daughter surprised me by announcing she had become a vegetarian. It was quite an announcement, coming as it did from a girl who had only ever eaten three types of vegetable in her life. It also threw my meal planning off completely as there wasn't much to offer her for dinner, except this soup. As it happened, it was a happy accident because she loved this and it has remained a firm favourite. This is a good one for all the family. When I have some cooked quinoa, which is often now there is a vegetarian in the house, I add some to each bowl before filling with soup.

Clara's minestrone

2–3 tablespoons extra virgin olive oil

1 onion, finely chopped

1 carrot, finely chopped

1 celery stick, finely chopped

1 leek, finely chopped

1 small courgette/zucchini, finely diced

75 g/¾ cup finely chopped mushrooms

1–2 garlic cloves, crushed

a splash of wine (optional)

1 litre/4 cups vegetable stock

a large handful of chopped fresh greens, such as spinach or blanched kale

a handful of chopped fresh basil leaves

250 ml/1 cup passata (Italian sieved tomatoes) or 227-g/8-oz can chopped tomatoes

60 g/½ cup trimmed and diced green beans

50 g/¼ cup tiny pasta stars

100 g/½ cup cooked quinoa (optional)

finely grated vegetarian Parmesan-style cheese, to serve

sea salt and black pepper

MAKES 4–6 SERVINGS

Heat the oil in a large saucepan and add the onion, carrot, celery, leek, courgette/zucchini and mushrooms. Cook over low heat for 8–10 minutes, stirring often. Season depending upon the salt content of your stock. (If in doubt, season gradually and taste frequently.) Stir in the garlic. Add the wine (if using) and cook for 1–2 minutes, until evaporated.

Stir in the stock and greens. Add the basil and passata. Bring to the boil, then lower the heat and simmer for at least 15 minutes, until all the vegetables are just tender. Taste and adjust the seasoning.

About 10 minutes before serving, bring the soup back to a simmer. Add the green beans and pasta. Simmer for about 10 minutes, until the pasta is tender. Taste for seasoning and adjust if necessary. Serve with the grated cheese for sprinkling.

Variation Add a small can of cooked, drained beans, such as cannellini or haricot/navy, after adding the pasta.

The amount of cooked barley required for this recipe is half the amount shown, but it makes good sense to prepare double the amount, while you're at it. The remaining half can be frozen, making it really quick to prepare this soup again in the future (or use the cooked barley for another recipe). This is a very basic preparation and offers a good way to introduce a nutritious and unusual grain into your child's diet. As it is so simple, it's a blueprint for quite a few quick and simple soups so be sure to look at the variations.

simple vegetable & barley soup

1–2 tablespoons extra virgin olive oil or rapeseed oil
1 small onion, finely chopped
1 small leek, halved and thinly sliced
1 carrot, quartered lengthwise and thinly sliced
1 celery stick, halved lengthwise and thinly sliced
1¼ litres/5 cups vegetable stock
100 g/½ cup barley, cooked according to package instructions and drained
sea salt and black pepper
a large handful of finely chopped fresh flat-leaf parsley leaves (optional)

MAKES 4–6 SERVINGS

Heat the oil in a large saucepan and add the onion, leek, carrot and celery. Cook over medium heat for about 5 minutes, until just soft. Season lightly, depending upon the salt content of your stock. If in doubt, season gradually and taste frequently. Add the stock, bring just to the boil, then lower the heat, cover and simmer gently for at least 15 minutes, until the vegetables are tender. Stir in half of the barley and the parsley (if using) and taste for seasoning. Add more water or stock if the soup is too thick. Serve hot.

Variations If you're really pushed for time, all of these can also be made without some or all of the base vegetables, so basically just the stock. Less nutrients but still wholesome.

Bean and barley soup Stir in a small can of drained and rinsed, cooked beans, such as borlotti, cannellini or haricot beans.

Mushroom and barley soup Add about 50 g/ ⅔ cup halved and thinly sliced mushrooms to the vegetables when softening. Replace 250 ml/1 cup of stock with milk.

Chunky potato and barley soup Replace 250 ml/1 cup stock with milk. Add a small cupful or so of finely diced cooked potato when adding the barley.

Rice, pea and tomato soup Omit the barley and stir in some cooked rice (about a cupful) and a large handful or so of frozen peas. To this also add a small can of chopped tomatoes, if liked. Serve with finely grated vegetarian cheese.

Spaghetti soup Omit the barley and add a small can of chopped tomatoes (or 250 ml/ 1 cup passata). Bring the soup to the boil. Take a small handful of spaghetti and break it into short pieces, letting it fall into the boiling soup. Serve with finely grated vegetarian cheese.

Italian egg soup Prepare the Spaghetti Soup (above) with or without the tomatoes. Whisk 2 eggs together in a bowl. Bring the soup to simmering point. Pour the eggs in, whisking constantly. You want strands of ribbon-like eggs, not clumps like scrambled. Cooked rice (about a cupful) can also replace the pasta here. Serve with finely grated vegetarian cheese.

This is a surprising combination of ingredients but a very pleasing one, and popular with young vegetarians. There is room to alter the seasonings according to taste by adding more or less curry powder and/or chilli. If nut allergies are a problem, omit the peanut butter and add a can of cooked drained chickpeas instead.

African peanut & sweet potato soup

2–3 tablespoons rapeseed oil

1 onion, chopped

2-cm/³⁄₄-in piece fresh ginger, peeled and grated

2 garlic cloves, crushed

¼ teaspoon dried chilli/hot pepper flakes (optional)

2 tablespoons curry powder

3 medium sweet potatoes, peeled and diced

227-g/8-oz can chopped tomatoes

1½ litres/6 cups vegetable stock

160 g/²⁄₃ cup smooth peanut butter

200 ml/³⁄₄ cup coconut milk

TO SERVE (OPTIONAL)

chopped coriander/cilantro

chopped unsalted peanuts

sea salt and black pepper

MAKES 4–6 SERVINGS

Heat 2 tablespoons oil in a large saucepan. Add the onion and cook over low heat for 5–8 minutes, until soft. Stir in the ginger, garlic, chilli/hot pepper flakes and curry powder and cook, stirring for 1–2 minutes more.

Stir in the sweet potatoes and tomatoes then add the stock. Simmer over low heat for about 20 minutes, until the sweet potatoes are tender. Taste and adjust the seasoning.

Stir in the peanut butter and coconut milk and simmer for 10 minutes more. Stir in the coriander/cilantro and peanuts (if using) and serve immediately.

Here is a basic recipe for a creamy tofu-based soup which makes a change from stock-based ones, and offers a good way to introduce protein-rich tofu into your child's diet.

creamy courgette soup

1 onion, finely chopped

1 courgette/zucchini, grated

1 tablespoon rapeseed oil

1 litre/4 cups vegetable stock

a large handful of chopped fresh flat-leaf parsley

250 ml/1 cup silken tofu or milk (or half and half)

sea salt and black pepper

MAKES 4–6 SERVINGS

Combine the courgette/zucchini, onion and oil in a large saucepan and cook for 3–5 minutes, until soft. Season lightly. Add the stock and parsley and simmer for 15–20 minutes, until the vegetables are tender. Stir in the tofu and cook to warm through. Taste and adjust the seasoning. Serve immediately.

A lifesaver for most parents, baked jacket potatoes represent an economical and healthy way to feed kids. If the potatoes are cooked in the microwave it is also a speedy way to put a meal on the table, but the skins will not be as crispy. An alternative to microwave cooking is to bake a batch in the oven and keep them in the fridge until needed; simply cut in half and use the microwave to warm up. Floury potatoes yield the nicest results when baked.

jacket potatoes

FILLING IDEAS

Veggie Chilli topped with sour cream (see page 126)

Vegetable Bolognese (see page 125)

Homemade Baked Beans (see page 89) topped with Houmous (see page 44)

steamed broccoli florets with any Pesto (see page 83)

Coleslaw (see page 48)

Sweet and Sour Tofu (see page 114)

Bean and Tofu Dip (see page 44)

Tofu Salad (see page 40)

sweetcorn with grated cheese

cottage cheese with diced tomato and chives

baked or sautéed mushrooms

sautéed thinly sliced leeks

ratatouille

Preheat the oven to 180ºC (350ºF) Gas 4.

Scrub the potatoes well and pat dry. Bake in the preheated oven (directly on the oven shelf) for 50–60 minutes. Remove when tender when pierced through with a skewer. Time depends on the size of the potato. If you use organic potatoes then encourage children to eat the skins as well, as this contains many nutrients. Serve with a green side salad, sliced cucumber rounds and/or carrot sticks. Many of the filling listed above (but not all) go well with the addition of grated vegetarian cheddar and/or a drizzle of cream.

This recipe is a 'stone soup' formula for dealing with a little bit of this, and a little bit of that all based around a single spud and a few veggie sausages. Another pulse/legume can be used, though lentils do work particularly well with potatoes.

skillet supper with lentils & veggie sausages

4 tablespoons extra virgin olive oil or rapeseed oil

1 onion, diced

1 yellow (bell) pepper, diced

150 g/1½ cups coarsely chopped mushrooms

½ teaspoon dried thyme

a pinch of dried chilli/hot pepper flakes (optional)

2–4 vegetarian sausages, sliced

1–2 garlic cloves, crushed

1 large waxy potato, diced

400-g/14-oz. can cooked lentils, drained and rinsed

400-g/14-oz. jar any tomato pasta sauce

sea salt and black pepper

MAKES 4 SERVINGS

Heat 2 tablespoons of the oil in a large deep frying pan/skillet with a lid. Add the onion and pepper and cook over low heat for 3–5 minutes, until just soft. Add the mushrooms, thyme, chilli/hot pepper flakes (if using) and the remaining oil and cook for a further 3–5 minutes, until the mushrooms begin to brown.

Add the sausages and cook until they begin to brown. Stir in the garlic and potato and cook for 1 minute more, stirring. Season lightly. Add the lentils and pasta sauce and stir well. You may need to add some water; the mixture should almost cover the potato pieces. Lower the heat, cover with a lid, and simmer gently for about 30 minutes, until the potatoes are tender.

Taste and adjust the seasoning. Remove the lid and simmer for 3–5 minutes to reduce the liquid a bit more. Serve immediately.

Here is a tasty sauce to whizz up and serve with noodles for a speedy bite, any time of day. This can be served immediately, but it is especially nice served cold, as a noodle salad, so make ahead and chill if there is time. For a more complete meal, serve with stir-fried cubes of firm tofu on top, accompany with a green vegetable, such as broccoli, and pass around the sweet chilli sauce.

noodles with sesame–peanut sauce

250 g/9 oz. oriental egg
  noodles or soba noodles
2–3 spring onions/scallions,
  sliced on the angle
2–3 tablespoons toasted
  sesame seeds

FOR THE SAUCE
4 tablespoons smooth
  peanut butter
30 g/¼ cup unsalted
  peanuts
leaves from a few sprigs
  of fresh basil
leaves from a sprig of
  fresh mint
leaves from a few sprigs of
  fresh coriander/cilantro
freshly squeezed juice of
  1 lime
65 ml/¼ cup rapeseed oil
1 tablespoon sesame oil
1–2 tablespoons sweet
  chilli sauce, to taste
2 tablespoons silken tofu
1–2 teaspoons soy sauce

MAKES 2–4 SERVINGS

To make the sauce, put the peanut butter, peanuts, basil, mint, coriander/cilantro, lime juice, both oils, chilli sauce, tofu and soy sauce in a food processor or blender and process to obtain a coarse paste. Taste and add more chilli sauce and/or soy sauce as required.

Cook the noodles according to the package instructions and drain well. Toss the sauce with the warm noodles and add the spring onions/scallions and sesame seeds. Serve warm or cold, as preferred.

Variation This sauce also makes a good dip for vegetables, either raw or lightly steamed. To serve, put the sauce in a small bowl and stir in the toasted sesame seeds. Offer a bowl of sweet chilli sauce alongside and a platter of prepared vegetables, such as broccoli, mangetout, carrots, sweet potato and red (bell) peppers.

SESAME SEEDS
Seeds in general, are a good source of healthy unsaturated fats. They provide poly-unsaturated fats which are thought to promote good health by offering a source of omega 6, as well as vitamins and minerals. In addition, sesame seeds are rich in the minerals copper and manganese and are also a good source of calcium. In the Middle East sesame seeds are ground into tahini, a thick paste which is a key component of houmous. Their flavour is improved by toasting.

Potatoes are popular, and potato recipes abound, but I find that many of them are cooked in the oven rather than on the stovetop. This is quite a nice, speedy stovetop method for making a meal out of a few potatoes, reminiscent of a traditional American recipe for hash, though this is meatless. The beans are optional if they are unwanted. This has slight Tex-Mex flavours and would go well with some tomato salsa and sour cream served on the side.

skillet potatoes with onions, beans, peppers & cheese

4–5 waxy potatoes, diced

2–4 tablespoons extra virgin olive oil or rapeseed oil

1 large onion, coarsely chopped

1 green or red (bell) pepper, diced

400-g/14-oz. can kidney beans, drained

a large handful of chopped fresh flat-leaf parsley (optional)

70 g/1 cup grated vegetarian cheddar, plus more to serve

sea salt and freshly ground black pepper

MAKES 4–6 SERVINGS

Put the potatoes in a large saucepan and cover with cold water. Bring to the boil, then lower the heat and simmer for about 10–20 minutes, until just barely tender when pierced with a fork. Drain and set aside.

Heat 2 tablespoon of the oil in a large frying pan/skillet. Add the onion and cook for about 3 minutes, until soft.

Add the pepper and potatoes and more oil if needed. Season well and toss to coat. Cook for 10–15 minutes, until well browned. Try not to stir too often or the potatoes will not brown – about once every 5 minutes or so is fine.

Taste and adjust the seasoning. Stir in the beans and parsley (if using) and cook for 2–3 minutes, just to warm through. Sprinkle the cheese on top and serve, with more grated cheese in a bowl to pass around.

Variation For adults or children with sophisticated palates, add ½ teaspoon ground cumin when cooking the onions. Stir in chopped olives and sliced jalapeño peppers (fresh or from a jar and drained) when adding the beans; use chopped fresh coriander/cilantro in place of the parsley. You could also add a fried egg on top of each serving as well, if liked.

This recipe comes from the Brittany region of France, where savoury crepes are commonplace. The traditional filling is a fried egg, cooked straight in the pan, on the cooked side after flipping the crepe. Moving away from tradition, these crepes can be filled with just about any savoury concoction you can imagine, but do try them with roast butternut squash pieces sprinkled with grated vegetarian cheese and drizzled with cream.

buckwheat crepes

200 g/1⅓ cups buckwheat flour
50 g/⅓ cup plain/all-purpose flour
125 ml/½ milk

2 eggs
a pinch of fine sea salt
unsalted butter, for cooking

MAKES ABOUT 12 CREPES

Put both the flours in a large mixing bowl and make a well in the middle. Put the milk in a measuring jug with 250 ml/1 cup water.

Break the eggs into the middle of the flour well and whisk them to blend. Gradually pour in the milk mixture, whisking constantly until just blended and smooth.

Cover and refrigerate. Let the batter rest; at least 15 minutes is manageable, 1 hour is acceptable and overnight is the best, if possible.

Preheat the oven to low; to keep the cooked crepes warm.

To cook the crepes, preheat a large non-stick skillet over medium high heat. Rub the pan with a knob of butter (use a wadded up piece of paper towel to do this, and keep reusing the same piece). Add a ladleful of batter to the middle of the pan and tilt, swirling to obtain as round a shape as possible. Cook until the edges begin to curl up and turn golden. Flip and cook the other side until golden. Transfer to a heatproof plate and put in the oven to keep warm. Continue cooking until all the batter is used up.

For many years, an omelette has been a regular evening meal in my house. Americans consider them a breakfast food, but they have a place on the dinner table too. The cooking technique is pretty straightforward but a non-stick pan is key, and start with high heat, but keep lowering as you cook.

perfect omelettes

2–3 eggs
a splash of milk
a pinch of fine sea salt

unsalted butter, for cooking

MAKES 1 SERVING

Crack the eggs into a bowl and whisk until frothy. Add the salt and milk and whisk to blend.

Heat a generous knob of butter in a small non-stick frying pan/skillet set over medium-high heat. When the butter is sizzling, pour in the eggs and lower the heat to medium-low. Cook, without disturbing the eggs for a few minutes, until a firm layer begins to set on the bottom. With a thin-edged rubber spatula, lift the edges of the omelette and tilt and swirl the pan so the runny egg from the top goes underneath to cook; try not to tear the firm layer which has already set. Do this all around the omelette, lower the heat near the end so the egg cooks but does not go too brown on the bottom. It should still be jiggly on top when filled.

To fill, imagine a line down the middle of the omelette, and place your chosen filling just the other side of the middle, on the side away from the handle (which will make it easier to slide onto the serving plate). Using the spatula, fold over to enclose the filling and slide onto the plate. Serve immediately.

Filling ideas In addition to the list for jacket potatoes on page 72, you could try: grated vegetarian cheddar; cream cheese; sautéed onions, peppers, mushrooms, courgettes/zucchini and/or leeks; avocado and tomato slices; cooked broccoli or asparagus; cooked greens, such as spinach, cabbage or kale, with some cream; or cooked sliced potatoes.

Here is a very simple and satisfying supper full of things most children love.

savoury sweetcorn pudding

1 tablespoon olive oil

1 large onion, finely chopped

600 ml/2½ cups milk

3 eggs, beaten

¼ teaspoon paprika

5–7 slices wholemeal/whole-wheat bread

300 g/2 cups sweetcorn kernels, fresh, frozen or canned

70 g/½ cup grated vegetarian cheddar

2–3 tablespoons grated Parmesan-style cheese

sea salt and black pepper

a 30 x 20-cm/12 x 8-in baking dish, generously buttered

MAKES 4–6 SERVINGS

Preheat the oven to 190°C (375°F) Gas 5.

Heat the oil in a frying pan/skillet. Add the onion and cook over low heat for 3–5 minutes, until soft. Set aside.

Combine the milk, eggs and paprika and season well. Whisk until well blended. Set aside.

Cut the bread slices into triangles and arrange them at an angle in the prepared baking dish and sprinkle over the sweetcorn and onions, lifting the bread to let some of the vegetable bits fall in between. Sprinkle over half of the cheddar, lifting the bread slices as before. Stir the remaining cheddar into the milk mixture and pour it over the bread. Sprinkle with the Parmesan-style cheese.

Bake in the preheated oven for about 30–40 minutes, until golden. Serve immediately.

Variation For Pizza Bread Pudding, omit the sweetcorn and replace with 3–4 tomatoes, halved and sliced. Arrange the tomato slices in between the bread slices, at random intervals. Sprinkle with a handful of sliced olives if liked. Omit the paprika and replace with 1 teaspoon dried oregano. Reduce the cheddar to 50 g/½ cup and stir it all into the milk mixture. Top with 1–2 mozzarellas, sliced. Drizzle with olive oil before baking.

These fritters make a wholesome meal when both time and energy are lacking.

cornmeal & sweetcorn fritters

160 g/1 cup cornmeal

40 g/¼ cup plain or wholemeal/whole-wheat flour

2 teaspoons baking powder

¼ teaspoon paprika

½ teaspoon fine sea salt

200 ml/¾ cup milk, plus more if needed

1 egg

300 g/2 cups sweetcorn kernels, fresh, frozen or canned

rapeseed oil and butter, for cooking

Applesauce (see page ooo), to serve (optional)

MAKES ABOUT 7 FRITTERS

Combine the cornmeal, flour, baking powder, paprika and salt in a large bowl and mix to combine. Measure out the milk in a measuring jug/pitcher, add the egg and whisk until blended. Pour the milk mixture into the cornmeal mixture and stir to blend. Stir in the sweetcorn kernels. Preheat the oven to low; just to keep the cooked fritters warm while you cook the others.

Heat some butter and oil in a large non-stick frying pan/skillet. When sizzling, add a ladleful of the batter to form one fritter. Only make as many at a time as fit comfortably in the pan. Cook for 3–5 minutes on one side, until browned. Turn and cook the other side until golden brown. Remove from the pan, drain on paper towels then transfer to a heatproof plate and put in the oven to keep warm while you prepare the rest. Serve immediately.

Variation For Thai-style Fritters, replace half the sweetcorn with thinly sliced spring onions/scallions, add a generous handful of chopped fresh coriander/cilantro and replace the paprika with 1 tablespoon grated fresh ginger; serve with sweet chilli sauce. For Tex-Mex Fritters, replace half the sweetcorn with diced green (bell) pepper and add ½ teaspoon ground cumin. Serve with tomato salsa and guacamole.

Pestos are a very good way of including nuts in a vegetarian diet. In addition to being delicious simply tossed with freshly cooked pasta, these also work as sandwich spreads or dips, either on their own or mixed with ricotta, yogurt or cream cheese.

pesto sauces
red pepper & walnut pesto

50 g/½ cup walnut pieces
100 g/½ cup sweet red peppers
   from a jar, drained
30 g/¼ cup grated Parmesan-
   style vegetarian cheese
leaves from a small bunch of
   fresh flat-leaf parsley
½ cup extra virgin olive oil or
   rapeseed oil

1 garlic clove, peeled
a drizzle of honey
1 tablespoon balsamic vinegar
freshly squeezed juice of
   ½ a lemon, or more to taste
sea salt and black pepper
2–3 tablespoons double/heavy
   cream, to serve (optional)

MAKES 375 ML/1¼ CUPS

Put all the ingredients in a food processor and blend to obtain a coarse paste. Taste and add more lemon juice, salt or pepper as required. If serving with pasta, add a few heaped spoonfuls of cream to the pasta along with the pesto when tossing together.

olive & almond pesto

75 g/½ cup almonds or cashews
60 g/½ cup pitted green olives
35 g/½ cup grated Parmesan-
   style vegetarian cheese
leaves from a few sprigs of
   fresh basil
¼–½ cup extra virgin olive oil
   or rapeseed oil

1 garlic clove, peeled
a drizzle of honey
freshly squeezed juice of
   ½ a lemon, or more to taste
sea salt and black pepper

MAKES 500–750 ML/2–3 CUPS

Put all the ingredients in a food processor. Blend to obtain a paste. Taste and add more lemon juice, salt or pepper as required.

broccoli & cashew pesto

30 g/¼ cup pine nuts
45 g/heaping ¼ cup cashews
florets from 1 small head of
   broccoli, steamed or boiled
35 g/½ cup grated Parmesan-
   style vegetarian cheese
a large handful of fresh
   basil leaves

¼ cup extra virgin olive oil
   or rapeseed oil
1 garlic clove, peeled
freshly squeezed juice of
   ½ a lemon, or more to taste
sea salt and black pepper

MAKES 500–750 ML/2–3 CUPS

Put all the ingredients in a food processor. Blend to obtain a paste. Taste and add more lemon juice, salt or pepper as required.

kids' favourites

These tasty burgers are great when you are feeding a crowd of your child's non-vegetarian friends. Serve them in toasted buns with lettuce, tomato slices, pickles, ketchup and mayonnaise with a bowl of hot fries on the side.

mushroom barley burgers

65 g/⅓ cup barley, rinsed and drained

1 slice wholemeal/ whole-wheat bread

1 small onion

2 tablespoons extra virgin olive oil

225 g/1¾ cups mushrooms, trimmed and halved

leaves from a few sprigs of fresh flat-leaf parsley

2 eggs

1 tablespoon soy sauce or tamari

50 g/½ cup grated vegetarian cheddar

1 tablespoon unsalted butter

sea salt and black pepper

TO SERVE (OPTIONAL)

9 wholemeal/whole-wheat buns or rolls

lettuce

tomato slices

ketchup

mayonaise

pickles

MAKES 9 BURGERS

Put the barley in a saucepan and add cold water to cover well. Add a pinch of salt and bring to the boil. Reduce the heat and simmer until tender 35–45 minutes. Drain and set aside.

Put the slice of bread in a food processor and process to obtain crumbs. Transfer to a bowl and set aside until needed.

Put the onion in the food processor and process to chop finely. Transfer to a non-stick frying pan/skillet, add 1 tablespoon of the oil and cook over low heat until soft.

Put the mushrooms and parsley in the food processor and process until finely chopped. Set aside until needed.

Crack the eggs into a mixing bowl, add a good pinch of salt and beat. Add the mushroom mixture, cooked barley, onions, breadcrumbs, soy sauce and cheese and mix well.

To cook, heat the butter and remaining oil in a large non-stick frying pan/skillet. Working in batches, drop clementine-size balls of the mushroom mixture into the pan and squash gently to flatten with the back of a spatula. Cook on one side for 3–4 minutes, until browned, then turn over and cook on the other side for 3–4 minutes more. Transfer to a plate. Serve hot in a bun with all the trimmings and fries or on their own with mashed potatoes, as preferred.

Reaching for a can of baked beans is a familiar gesture for many parents – it's cheap, nutritious, quick and popular with children. As making them from scratch seems fairly unachievable given the pace of modern family life, this simplified recipe is designed as a compromise between the processed option and simmering the real thing for hours. In an unofficial taste test, involving young people eating at my home one evening, this was rated as on par with the leading canned variety. High praise indeed.

homemade baked beans

410-g/14-oz. can haricot/navy beans (no salt and sugar added), rinsed and drained
125 ml/½ cup unsweetened apple juice
1 teaspoon cider vinegar
2 tablespoons ketchup

1 teaspoon dark brown sugar, honey or agave syrup
1 teaspoon vegetarian Worcestershire sauce
sea salt

MAKES 2 MAIN COURSE SERVINGS OR 4 SIDE DISH SERVINGS

Combine all the ingredients in a large saucepan and add a pinch of salt. Stir well. Cover and simmer for 25 minutes. Taste and adjust the seasoning, adding more salt or apple juice as required.

Simmer, uncovered, for 10–20 minutes, until the liquid has reduced and thickened. Taste for seasoning. Serve immediately.

Note It took several tries to get this right and a large part of the problem was the quality of the canned beans. The best version was made with organic haricot/navy beans, as these had the desired meltingly tender baked-bean like texture. You may need to experiment to find the right brand of bean available to you.

This is basic and not terribly authentic, but children seem to like the flavours. It is certainly very quick and easy to prepare as well as being nutritious.

bbq bean tacos

410-g/14-oz. can kidney or pinto beans, drained and rinsed
1 tablespoon barbecue sauce
1 tablespoon ketchup
195-g/7-oz. can sweetcorn kernels, drained

5–6 cherry tomatoes, chopped
1 little gem lettuce, washed, dried and shredded
grated vegetarian cheddar, to serve
corn taco shells or flour tortillas

MAKES 4–6 SERVINGS

Combine the beans, barbecue sauce and ketchup in a small saucepan. Cook, stirring, until the beans are warmed through.

Arrange all the other ingredients in separate bowls. Warm the taco shells or tortillas according to the package instructions.

To serve, spoon some of the bean mixture into each taco shell or tortilla. Pass round the bowls of toppings for the children to assemble their own.

The longer you marinate the tofu the more flavourful it becomes – overnight is best. You may want to make additional noodle sauce to offer for dipping, or just use plain soy or tamari. To make this more adult friendly, sliced fresh red chillies and a splash of mirin can be added to the noodle sauce, as well as a sprinkling of toasted sesame seeds. You can simply serve these as fingers or, after cooking, skewer the tofu on an ice lolly/popsicle stick – wooden skewers seem too pointed to offer to kids, but they should look like kebabs/kabobs.

tofu kebabs with noodles

FOR THE KEBABS/KABOBS
200 g/7 oz. firm tofu, pressed (see page 94) and cut into fingers
1 tablespoon runny honey
1 tablespoon Dijon mustard
1 tablespoon soy sauce
45 g/1 cup fresh wholemeal/whole-wheat breadcrumbs
a large pinch of paprika
1 teaspoon fine sea salt
rapeseed oil, for cooking

FOR THE NOODLES
200 g/7 oz. fine oriental egg noodles
1 tablespoon vegetable oil
1 tablespoon honey
60 ml/¼ cup orange juice or apple juice
3–4 tablespoons soy sauce or tamari
spring onions/scallions, to serve (optional)

MAKES 2–4 SERVINGS

Arrange the tofu fingers in a dish which is just large enough to hold them in a single layer.

If necessary, soften the honey in a microwave for 10–20 seconds, just so it blends well with the other marinade ingredients. In a small bowl, combine the honey, mustard and soy sauce and mix well. Pour over the tofu and coat the tofu on all sides. Cover with clingfilm/plastic wrap and refrigerate until needed – up to 24 hours and for at least 30 minutes.

When ready to cook the tofu, season the breadcrumbs with the paprika and salt. Spread them over a plate. Remove the tofu from the marinade and pat dry lightly with paper towels. Transfer each finger to the breadcrumbs and turn to coat on all sides, pressing the crumbs into the tofu. Transfer to a clean plate.

Heat 2–3 tablespoons oil (enough to cover the bottom of the pan) in a non-stick frying pan/skillet. Add the tofu and cook for about 2 minutes, until just browned. Turn carefully with tongs and continue cooking about 2 minutes on each side, until browned all over. Transfer to a plate lined with paper towels, insert a stick into each one and set aside.

Cook the noodles according to the package instructions. Drain, toss with the oil to prevent sticking. Combine the honey, orange juice and soy sauce in a large frying pan/skillet. Heat and stir to blend. Add the cooked noodles and toss to coat them in the sauce. Cook over low heat just until warmed through.

Serve the tofu kebabs/kabobs with the noodles and some green beans. Offer additional noodle sauce or soy sauce for dipping, as preferred, and serve with shredded spring onions/scallions, if liked.

This is loads of fun and a great way to get vegetables into a crowd of children. You do not need a fondue pot but, obviously, that is a bonus. I use an enamel-coated saucepan for this and it works just fine. Most vegetarian hard cheeses are suitable but the cheese spread is the secret ingredient. It does something inexplicably wonderful to the taste and gives it a creamy, unctuous texture. For a grown-up version of the same thing, use more sophisticated cheeses, and replace the apple juice with white wine.

cheery fondue

juice of ½ a lemon
250 ml/1 cup apple juice
2 teaspoons cornflour/ cornstarch
300 g/2½ cups grated vegetarian cheddar and/or Gruyère
1 portion cheese spread, such as Laughing Cow

TO SERVE
cubes of bread
boiled baby new potatoes
steamed broccoli and/or cauliflower florets
oven-roasted slices of butternut squash or sweet potato

MAKES 6–8 SERVINGS

Combine the lemon juice and apple juice in a large saucepan. Heat briefly, then stir in the cornflour/ cornstarch until dissolved. Add the grated cheese and the cheese spread and cook, stirring often, until fully melted.

Serve straight from the pan, taking care that the children do not touch the sides of the pan. Alternatively, transfer to a heatproof glass bowl and serve.

Note The fondue will need occasional warming to keep the consistency right for dipping. Return the pan to the heat and stir to rewarm. If using a bowl, keep a pan of water simmering gently on the stovetop and set the glass bowl on top, stirring to warm. The bowl will become warm so, again, take care with the children.

Growing up, mealtimes were often a fraught experience. My mother had four children to contend with, an incredibly fussy bunch when it came to food and, to make matters worse, most of us liked different things from one another. Sound familiar? Bread Loaf BBQ was the one thing we all loved so, herewith, a fantastic vegetarian version.

bread loaf bbq

1 onion, coarsely chopped

1 red (bell) pepper, coarsely chopped

1 celery stick, chopped

2 tablespoons extra virgin olive oil or vegetable oil

2 garlic cloves, crushed

400 ml/1²/₃ cups passata (Italian sieved tomatoes)

2 teaspoons vegetarian Worcestershire sauce

1 teaspoon dried oregano

1 teaspoon ground cumin

1 tablepoon ketchup

1 tablepoon cider vinegar

1 generous tablespoon dark brown sugar

2 tablespoons barbecue sauce

400 g/14 oz. firm tofu, pressed (see right) and crumbled

400-g/14-oz. bread loaf

grated vegetarian cheese, to serve (optional)

sea salt and black pepper

MAKES 4–6 SERVINGS

Put the onion, red pepper and celery in a food processor and blend until minced. Alternatively, chop very finely.

Combine in a large frying pan/skillet with the oil and cook until soft, stirring often. Add the garlic and cook for 1 minute. Stir in the passata, Worcestershire sauce, oregano, cumin, ketchup, vinegar, sugar and barbecue sauce. Let simmer for 10 minutes. Taste and adjust the seasoning. Stir in the tofu and simmer, covered, for about 15–20 minutes more.

Meanwhile, slice the top off the loaf and set aside. Hollow out the loaf by pulling out the soft bread, shred and stir into the tofu mixture.

Preheat the oven to 200°C (400°F) Gas 6.

Set the bread loaf on a piece of kitchen foil large enough to wrap around the bread. Fill the hollow loaf with the tofu mixture and replace the bread lid. Enclose with the foil and bake in the preheated oven for 20 minutes.

Remove from the oven and serve, with grated cheese, if liked.

Variation For Tofu Sloppy Joes, omit the loaf and replace with bread rolls or hamburger buns. Do not hollow the bread, simply serve the tofu mixture piled on the halved rolls.

PRESSING TOFU

Tofu needs to be pressed to extract moisture before cooking for a better texture and I am grateful to my MSc dissertation tutor for sharing her tofu tips with me. In any recipe which calls for firm tofu, before using, remove the tofu from its packaging. Set in a dish (not a plate since liquid will be extracted) and place a small, clean plate on top. Set a few cans (canned beans are good) on the plate to weight down the tofu, making sure the sides of the dish do not prevent the weight from pressing down on the tofu. Let stand at least 15 minutes before using, but longer is fine. Drain the excess liquid, then use as required.

As a non-vegetarian, I have struggled with the notion of a nut loaf, but The Cookery School in central London, where I work, has a recipe for the most delicious one ever, which made me a convert and I have adapted it here. As with everything they do, the beauty lies in the simplicity. There are not too many fussy ingredients or complicated procedures, just whizz up this mixture using quality products and it will taste fantastic. Try it for yourself and see.

nutty meatballs

250 g/2½ cups mixed nuts (walnuts, cashews, almonds and chestnuts)

100 g/generous 1½ cups wholemeal/whole-wheat breadcrumbs

2 medium onions, peeled and quartered

1 celery stick

1 small carrot

2–3 garlic cloves, peeled

leaves from a small bunch of fresh flat-leaf parsley

3–5 tablespoons olive oil

1 teaspoon dried thyme

2 teaspoons vegetable bouillon powder

1 egg, beaten

1–2 tablespoons milk

sea salt and black pepper

TO SERVE (OPTIONAL)

1 quantity Basic Tomato Sauce (see page 98)

wholemeal/whole-wheat spaghetti or penne

finely grated Parmesan-style vegetarian cheese

MAKES 4–6 SERVINGS

Preheat the oven to 180ºC (350ºF) Gas 4.

Put the nuts in the bowl of the food processor and process until finely ground. Add to the breadcrumbs, season lightly and set aside.

Put the onions, celery, carrot, garlic cloves and parsley in the food processor and process until finely chopped.

Heat 3 tablespoons of the oil in a large frying pan/skillet. Add the onion mixture and thyme, season and cook for 5–7 minutes, until softened. Remove from the heat and let cool slightly.

Add the onion mixture to the nut mixture and stir well. Dissolve the bouillon powder in 125 ml/½ cup hot water and add to the onion mixture. Stir well. Add the egg and mix to combine. If the mixture is very dry, add the milk, or some water, 1 tablespoon at a time. The mixture needs to be soft or the finished dish will be dry, but not too soft.

Use your hands to shape the mixture into golf ball-size balls and arrange them on a baking sheet. Bake in the preheated oven for about 35 minutes, until browned. Serve in warmed tomato sauce with pasta and finely grated cheese, if liked.

Variations For Nut Fritters, shape the mixture into small rounds (starting from the same golf ball size) flatten slightly, then pan-fry until browned on both sides. Alternatively, for a Nut Loaf, transfer the mixture to a non-stick loaf tin/pan and bake for 35–40 minutes, until browned on top.

For an easy life, make this pie in whatever shape the puff pastry sheets come in, usually a rectangle. Alternatively, use a small bowl to trace out pastry circles, fill with vegetable mixture, fold over and seal to enclose for individual vegetable turnovers. More fussy and time consuming to prepare, but children will enjoy helping with the preparations. The spinach is optional; it can be omitted if unavailable or disliked. This is a great recipe for feeding a crowd of kids or the entire family, with steamed new potatoes and a green salad on the side.

vegetable pie

2 sheets ready-made all-butter puff pastry

3–4 large mushrooms, quartered and sliced

1 red or yellow (bell) pepper, diced

200 g/1 cup sweetcorn kernels (fresh or canned)

150-g/6-oz. can beans, such as borlotti, cannellini or pinto, drained and rinsed

75 g/3 cups fresh baby spinach leaves, washed and dried (optional)

80 g/²/₃ cup grated vegetarian cheddar

2–3 tablespoons milk, for glazing

BASIC TOMATO SAUCE

1 small onion, chopped

1 celery stick, chopped

1–2 tablespoons olive oil

2 garlic cloves, finely chopped

1 teaspoon fine sea salt

a splash of wine (optional)

225-g/8 oz. can chopped tomatoes

a pinch of sugar

MAKES 8–10 SERVINGS

To make the tomato sauce, combine the onion, celery and oil in a frying pan/skllet and cook until soft. Add the garlic and cook for 1 minute. Season with salt and add the wine (if using). Stir and cook until evaporated. Add the tomatoes and sugar and stir. Cook for at least 15 minutes. Taste for seasoning, adjust as required and set aside until needed.

Preheat the oven to 200ºC (400ºF) Gas 6.

Line a baking sheet with one of the pastry sheets, leaving at least 1-cm/½-inch overhang on all sides. Spread with the tomato sauce in an even layer. Arrange the mushrooms, pepper, sweetcorn, beans, spinach (if using) and cheese on top of the sauce.

Cover with the remaining pastry sheet, fold the bottom edge over and push down to seal. Brush the top with milk to glaze. Cut a series of slits at an angle in the top starting in one corner and working across, to allow steam to escape.

Bake in the preheated oven for 25–30 minutes, until browned. Serve warm with boiled or steamed new potatoes and a salad, if liked.

This is the meal of choice for many an American child and there are also a fair few adults who share this sentiment. With good reason; it is delicious but, alas, boxed preparations are what most kids know because this is how so many busy parents cook. Making this from scratch is no big deal. This recipe has the advantage of built-in vegetables which, when coated in a cheese sauce, seem to go down relatively easily. Unlike other pasta recipes in this book, this does not call for wholemeal/whole-wheat pasta. Far better to get box-fed kids enjoying this first but, if you have the luxury of serving this to kids who have never had it from a box and who are used to wholemeal pasta then, by all means, carry on.

mac 'n cheese with spinach

50 g/3½ tablespoons butter

3 tablespoons plain/ all-purpose flour

600 ml/2⅓ cups milk

100 g/1½ cups grated vegetarian cheddar, or more if liked

150 g/1 cup frozen spinach, defrosted

300 g/3 cups macaroni

3–4 tablespoons wholemeal/whole-wheat breadcrumbs

sea salt and black pepper

a 30 x 20-cm/12 x 8-inch baking dish, generously buttered

MAKES 6–8 SERVINGS

Preheat the oven to 190ºC (375ºF) Gas 5.

Melt the butter in a saucepan set over medium heat. Add the flour and cook, stirring constantly with a wooden spoon, for 1 minute. Gradually add the milk, stirring continuously, and cook for about 5 minutes, until the sauce thickens.

Season lightly, add the cheese and stir until melted. Remove from the heat and stir in the spinach. Taste and adjust the seasoning. Add more grated cheese, to taste.

Cook the macaroni according to the package instructions and drain. Put in the prepared dish and pour over the sauce. Mix well to combine and spread evenly. Sprinkle the breadcrumbs on top and bake in the preheated oven for 20–30 minutes, until bubbling. Serve hot.

Variation Other vegetables can be used in place of the spinach and frozen, defrosted vegetables work especially well here. Try sweetcorn kernels, broccoli and cauliflower florets and mixed diced vegetables. Older children may enjoy 1–2 sautéed leeks in place of the spinach.

Polenta is classic Italian cornmeal, which is cooked into a kind of porridge. For this recipe you need the quick-cook version, as it can be prepared very speedily. It is used here to cover oven-roasted vegetables and topped with melting mozzarella, to make a comforting and nutritious pie kids will love.

cheesy polenta & roasted vegetable pie

2 small courgettes/zucchini

1 red (bell) pepper

1 yellow (bell) pepper

300 g/10 oz. broccoli, sliced into long thin 'trees'

1 red onion, sliced into thick rings

200 g/1⅓ cups polenta

1 tablespoon butter

80 g/⅔ cup grated vegetarian cheddar

125-g/4½-oz. mozzarella ball, sliced

extra virgin olive oil

sea salt

a 25-cm/10-inch square or round baking dish, greased

MAKES 6–8 SERVINGS

Preheat the oven to 200°C (400°F) Gas 6.

Cut the courgettes/zucchini in half widthwise, then halve lengthwise and cut into long thin fingers. Seed the peppers then cut into thick slices. Spread the vegetables in a single layer on a baking sheet and add the broccoli and onion. Drizzle over 2–3 tablespoons oil and toss to coat. Season lightly with salt and roast in the preheated oven for 10–20 minutes, until just tender and lightly browned. You may need to roast in batches, depending on the size of your vegetables, and the broccoli may cook quicker. Check after 15 minutes and remove it if necessary, continue cooking the other vegetables. Remove from the oven and transfer to the prepared dish.

Put 800 ml/3¼ cups water in a large saucepan, season lightly and add the polenta in a stream. Cook, whisking constantly, until thick. Take care

as polenta can bubble up a bit ferociously. When thick, lower the heat and continue cooking, stirring constantly, for 5 minutes more.

Remove from the heat, stir in the butter and grated cheddar. Pour over the vegetables in the dish and spread out evenly with a spatula. Arrange the mozzarella slices on top and bake in the preheated oven for about 25 minutes, until browned and bubbling. Serve hot.

Variation For a quick and easy meal, bake the polenta in a generously buttered tin/pan without the vegetables and serve it in slices with a Basic Tomato Sauce (see page 98) and any steamed green vegetables of your choice.

family feasts

Having discovered that beans go down better when puréed, I've sought to collect as many puréed bean recipes as possible and this one has proved immensely popular with all age groups. You can use almost any cooked bean you like here – choose from cannellini, kidney, haricot/ navy or butter beans. It is also a good way to serve an unusual and highly nutritious grain.

150 g/1 cup unroasted
   buckwheat groats
2 x 410-g/14-oz. cans beans
1 onion, coarsely chopped
165 ml/³⁄₄ cup thick cream
1 garlic clove, crushed
2 tablespoons sun-dried
   tomato paste
1 teaspoon dried thyme
3 tomatoes, coarsely chopped
70 g/1 cup grated vegetarian
   cheddar
¼ teaspoon paprika
2 eggs, beaten
chopped fresh flat-leaf
   parsley, to serve (optional)
sea salt and black pepper

6–8 individual tartlet tins/pan

MAKES 6–8 MINI QUICHES

bean, cheese & tomato quiches with a buckwheat crust

Preheat the oven to 200°C (400°F) Gas 6.

Put the buckwheat in a large saucepan and add 300 ml/1½ cups cold water. Bring to the boil, then reduce the heat and simmer, uncovered, for 7 minutes. Remove from the heat, cover and let stand until all the water has been absorbed.

Meanwhile, put the beans in a food processor with the onion and cream and process until smooth. Transfer to a mixing bowl and stir in the garlic, sun-dried tomato paste, thyme, tomatoes, cheese and paprika. Season well, then mix to blend. Taste and adjust the seasoning, then stir in the eggs. Set aside until needed.

As soon as the buckwheat is cool enough to handle, press it into the tins/pans, going up the sides, to form a crust. Transfer to a baking sheet and pour in the bean mixture. Bake in the preheated oven for 25–35 minutes, until firm but still wobbly in the middle. Sprinkle with chopped parsley and serve warm with a salad.

Variation If preferred you can bake this as one large tart in a generously buttered 23-cm/ 9-inch tart tin/pan with a removable base.

The idea for this recipe was inspired by a friend, whose children love the onion pie she makes. Her recipe calls for shortcrust pastry but the day I was testing this, I ran out of ready-made pastry and time was too short to make pastry from scratch. Having just made a batch of scones and with all the ingredients in front of me, I simply made the dough again and plopped it on top of the onions. Easier than pastry and very tasty too! This makes for a wholesome and satisfying week-day supper and is ideal served with a green vegetable or a salad, with some fresh fruit and yogurt for dessert.

onion pie

5–6 large onions (a mix of red and white)

2–3 tablespoons extra virgin olive oil

leaves from a few sprigs of fresh thyme

125 g/1 cup plain/ all-purpose flour

125 g/1 cup wholemeal/ whole-wheat flour

1 generous teaspoon baking powder

¼ teaspoon fine sea salt

75 g/5 tablespoons unsalted butter at room temperature, cut into pieces

150 ml/scant ⅓ cup milk

an enamel-coated ovenproof frying pan/skillet or a non-stick cake pan/tin

MAKES 6–8 SERVINGS

Preheat the oven to 200°C (400°F) Gas 6.

Heat the oil in the frying pan/skillet. (If using an ovenproof skillet, you can cook the onions and bake the pie in the same pan. Alternatively, cook the onions in a non-stick frying pan/skillet, then transfer to a cake tin/pan.) When hot, add the onions and thyme and cook over medium heat for 5–8 minutes, stirring occasionally, until soft and lightly browned. Season well. Set aside while you prepare the scone dough.

Put both flours, baking powder and salt in a mixing bowl. Add the butter and rub in with your fingertips to obtain coarse crumbs. Add the milk and stir to obtain a soft dough. Transfer to a lightly floured surface and roll out to a round just larger than the diameter of the pan.

Transfer the dough to the pan, tucking it in around the edges to enclose the onions. Make a few slits in the dough with a sharp knife to allow steam to escape during baking.

Bake in the preheated oven for 20–25 minutes, until the dough is firm and cooked. Let cool for a few minutes, then turn the pie over and cut into slices to serve.

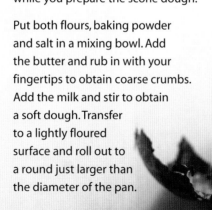

Vegetable crumbles have long been a staple of British vegetarian cuisine and a friend recently recalled how, in the 1970s, she prepared many a crumble for her young vegetarian brother because her mother could not cope with meatless cooking. I looked up the original recipe from the legendary Cranks Cookbook, and then set about updating it. This is the result, using butternut squash, virtually unknown in 1970s Britain but very popular now, especially with children. This is also inspired by a traditional Provençal recipe, which combines pumpkin purée, rice and béchamel sauce.

butternut squash & chestnut crumble

1-kg/2-lb. butternut squash

150 g/1 cup chestnuts, roughly chopped

225 g/1 cup brown rice, cooked

150 g/1 stick plus 2½ tablespoons butter

3 tablespoons plain/ all-purpose flour

600 ml/2⅓ cups milk

70 g/1 cup grated vegetarian cheddar

175 g/1 cup wholemeal/ whole-wheat flour

2 tablespoons each pumpkin seeds and sunflower seeds

3 tablespoons finely grated Parmesan-style vegetarian cheese

a pinch of fine sea salt

an ovenproof baking dish, generously buttered

MAKES 4–6 SERVINGS

Preheat the oven to 190°C (375°F) Gas 5.

Peel and deseed the squash and cut it into large chunks. Put in the prepared baking dish with the chestnuts and cooked rice and toss gently to combine. Set aside.

To make the sauce, melt 50 g/3½ tablespoons of the butter in a saucepan set over medium heat. Stir in the flour and cook for 1 minute, stirring constantly. Gradually add the milk, and cook for about 5 minutes, stirring constantly, until thickened. Season lightly and stir in the cheddar until melted. Taste and adjust the seasoning.

Pour the sauce over the squash mixture and mix to coat the vegetables in the sauce.

To make the crumble topping, combine the remaining butter with the flour, seeds, cheese and salt in a food processor and process just to mix. Sprinkle the crumble mixture over the squash, distributing it evenly, but patchily – it should not form a solid covering.

Bake in the preheated oven for 30–40 minutes, until bubbling. Serve hot or warm.

There is something very pleasing about the texture of orzo pasta and it marries well with the courgette/zucchini (which practically disappears in the sauce so this is a good one if hidden vegetables are required.) This dish is ideal for a crowd and can be a meal in itself, or accompany it with a mixed bean salad. Alternatively, stir in a drained can of haricot/navy beans or chickpeas and serve with a fresh tomato salad to make this more nutritionally complete.

creamy orzo pasta bake

250 g/2 cups orzo
  (rice-shaped pasta)
400 ml/1²/₃ cups double/
  heavy cream or crème
  fraîche
1 courgette/zucchini,
  roughly grated
a large handful of chopped
  fresh flat-leaf parsley
  leaves (optional)
finely grated zest of
  ½ a lemon
50 g/½ cup grated hard
  vegetarian cheese (such
  as cheddar or emmental),
  or crumbled feta
sea salt and black pepper

a 30 x 20-cm/12 x 8-inch
ovenproof baking dish,
greased or buttered

MAKES 6–8 SERVINGS

Preheat the oven to 200ºC (400ºF) Gas 6.

Cook the orzo according to the package instructions, drain well and transfer to a mixing bowl. Pour in the cream or créme fraîche and add the courgette/zucchini, parsley (if using) and lemon zest. Mix well until thoroughly combined. Season well and transfer to the prepared baking dish. Spread evenly and sprinkle over the cheese.

Bake in the preheated oven for about 20–30 minutes, until just browned. Serve immediately with a bean or tomato salad.

Variation For a Tomato Orzo Pasta Bake, omit the cream and lemon zest and prepare the Basic Tomato Sauce on page 98, replacing the tomatoes with 700 ml/2³/₄ cups passata (Italian sieved tomatoes). Combine the sauce with the cooked orzo. Add the courgette/zucchini and parsley (if using). Mix well to blend. Season lightly and transfer to a baking dish. Spread evenly, sprinkle with grated vegetarian cheese and bake as for the main recipe.

This combination of vegetables offers a pleasing mix of colours, tastes and textures but you could just as easily make this with a different combination or even a single vegetable. Cauliflower or broccoli are both especially nice when served in a creamy baked gratin, and they should be blanched beforehand like the greens in this recipe. Serve with wholegrains or a mixed bean salad.

mixed vegetable gratin with tofu

200 g/2 cups sliced greens, such as cabbage or spinach

1 leek, thinly sliced

1 large carrot, grated

1 sweet potato, finely chopped or coarsely grated

400 ml/1²/₃ cups single/light cream or crème fraîche

100 g/4 oz. silken tofu

1 egg

3–4 tablespoons finely grated Parmesan-style vegetarian cheese

3–4 tablespoons breadcrumbs

a 30 x 20-cm/12 x 8-inch baking dish, generously buttered

MAKES 6 SERVINGS

Preheat the oven to 200°C (400°F) Gas 6.

Bring a large saucepan of water to the boil. Add the greens and cook for 1–2 minutes, just to blanch. Drain. Combine the blanched greens, leek, carrot and sweet potato in the prepared baking dish. Season well and mix to blend.

Combine the cream, tofu and egg in a food processor and process until smooth. Pour over the vegetables. Sprinkle with the grated cheese, then sprinkle over the breadcrumbs.

Bake in the preheated oven for 30–40 minutes, until bubbling. Serve immediately.

This dish is ideal if you are trying to introduce tofu; the sauce is fresh, tangy and surprisingly tasty. If tofu is not appreciated, it can be omitted and replaced with steamed broccoli florets, mangetout or green beans tossed in the sauce to warm before serving. Serve with rice and a green vegetable, if liked.

sweet & sour tofu

1 tablespoon vegetable oil

1 medium onion, cut in 2-cm/³/₄-inch pieces

1 red (bell) pepper, cut in 2-cm/³/₄-inch pieces

1 carrot, sliced into thin rounds

1 celery stick, cut in 2-cm/ ³/₄-inch pieces

1 teaspoon plain/all-purpose flour

225-g/8-oz. can pineapple chunks, drained and juice reserved

125 ml/ ½ cup apple juice

125 ml/½ cup ketchup

1 tablespoon soy sauce

1–3 teaspoons cider vinegar

350-g/12 oz. tofu, pressed (see page 94) and cubed

cooked rice, to serve

MAKES 3–4 SERVINGS

Combine the oil, onion and pepper in a frying pan/skillet with a lid and cook for about 3 minutes, until just beginning to soften. Add the carrot and celery and continue cooking for 5–10 minutes more, stirring often, until just tender.

Stir in the flour and cook for 1 minute. Add the reserved pineapple juice, apple juice, ketchup, soy sauce and 1 teaspoon of the vinegar. Mix well, cover and let simmer for 5 minutes.

Gently stir in the pineapple chunks and the tofu. Cover and cook over low heat for 3–5 minutes, just to warm through. Time permitting, let stand, covered, for about 30 minutes to allow the tofu to absorb all the flavours and reheat gently before serving. Alternatively, serve immediately with rice.

Any vegetables can be used for this dish but in my experience children especially like the sweetness of butternut squash and parsnips, and the roasted pears continue the theme. To maintain a healthy rainbow of colours, serve with red and green foods, such as cherry tomatoes, strawberries, grapes, cucumber; whatever is to hand or in season.

roasted vegetable & fruit fingers with couscous

2 tablespoons unsalted butter

2–3 tablespoons extra virgin olive oil

1 small butternut squash, peeled and cut into bite-size pieces

2 parsnips, peeled and sliced lengthwise

2 pears, cored and sliced lengthwise (peeled if preferred)

a few pinches of sea salt

COUSCOUS

200 g/1 cup wholemeal/ whole-wheat couscous

300 g/2 cups peas (fresh or frozen)

1 tablespoon extra virgin olive oil

MAKES 3–4 SERVINGS

Preheat the oven to 200ºC (400ºF) Gas 6.

Melt the butter in a small heatproof bowl in the microwave. Stir in the oil and set aside.

Arrange the squash, parsnips and pears in a single layer on a baking sheet and brush with the butter mixture. Sprinkle the squash and parsnips lightly with salt. Roast in the preheated oven for about 25 minutes, until golden and tender, turning after about 10–15 minutes and brushing with more of the butter mixture. You may need to work in batches.

Prepare the couscous according to the package instructions. Cook the peas, drain and add to the couscous Stir in the oil.

To serve, divide the roasted vegetables and fruit among the plates and accompany with a mound of the couscous.

Variation Replace the peas with a 410-g/14-oz can of drained and rinsed chickpeas and a large handful of sultanas/golden raisins, that have been plumped up in boiling water.

This has a lovely sweet-sour flavour which appeals to many children, assuming they can get past the red cabbage part! It goes well with the potato pancakes (right) and many other kinds of potato dish, as well as with vegetarian sausages. The taste improves with time so this is a good dish to make in advance.

braised red cabbage with apples, raisins & chestnuts

1 onion, halved and sliced
2–4 tablespoons vegetable oil
800 g/about 8 cups thinly sliced
    red cabbage
½ teaspoon ground cinnamon
½ teaspoon ground allspice
1 kg/2 lbs. tart eating apples,
    peeled and chopped
75g/⅓ cup plus 2 tablespoons
    raisins

200 g/2 cups chestnuts
    (optional)
250 ml/1 cup apple juice
200 ml/¾ cup passata (Italian
    sieved tomatoes)
3 tablespoons ketchup
1–2 tablespoons cider vinegar
a pinch of sugar (optional)
sea salt and black pepper

MAKES 4–6 SERVINGS

Combine the onion and 2 tablespoons of the oil in a frying pan/skillet with a lid and cook for about 3 minutes, until soft. Add the cabbage, spices, apples and raisins and more oil if needed. Toss to blend and cook for 2–3 minutes more. Stir in the chestnuts and season.

Add the apple juice, passata, ketchup and 1 tablespoon of the vinegar. Mix well and bring to a simmer. Taste and adjust the seasoning. Cover and simmer gently for about 30 minutes, until the cabbage is tender. Add more apple juice if the mixture is dry and continue to simmer for 15 minutes more. Taste and add more vinegar or sugar, according to taste. Serve immediately.

Although a short recipe, this is perhaps the most time consuming recipe in the book. Don't be put off, this is very easy and very delicious. These just need to be cooked to order and eaten almost as soon as they come out of the pan.

potato pancakes with applesauce

500 g/1 lb. floury potatoes
    (baking potatoes are good)
butter and vegetable oil,
    for frying
a pinch of fine sea salt

APPLESAUCE
1–2 large, tart cooking apples,
    peeled and diced
apple juice (optional)
1–2 tablespoons sugar

MAKES 8–10 PANCAKES

To make the applesauce, put the apple pieces in a saucepan and add sufficient water to almost cover (or use apple juice, in which case you may need to sweeten less, or not at all). Cover and cook over medium heat, stirring occasionally until the apple is cooked through and very tender. Taste and add sugar as required. Some cooking apples dissolve well when cooked and can simply be mashed up with a wooden spoon, others do not. If you want a very smooth purée, you may need to whizz in a food processor. Set aside while you make the potato pancakes.

Work in batches, making two pancakes each time. If you grate the potatoes too far in advance they will discolour so grate as you go. Grate one potato, pat dry with paper towels to remove excess moisture and season with a little salt. Melt about 1 tablespoon of butter in a non-stick frying pan/skillet and add sufficient oil to coat the bottom of the pan. When hot, add half the grated potato and, using a wooden spoon, tap and shape into a pancake. Repeat with the remaining grated potato. Cook both pancakes for 3–5 minutes, until well browned, then turn and cook the other side for 3–5 minutes more. (Cooking time will depend on size and thickness.) While the second side is cooking, start grating and drying the next potato. Serve immediately with the applesauce.

An important aspect to consider when feeding vegetarian children is maintaining a balance of grains in their diet. Barley is a good grain and this is an interesting way to serve it. The method is identical to making risotto with rice so nothing really new here, except the ingredients. Try other vegetables with the carrots or as a replacement: celery, peppers and mushrooms are all good, and you can always throw in a handful of frozen peas, just give them a few minutes to defrost and warm through before serving. Serve this with a bean salad.

barley risotto with carrots

300 g/1½ cups barley
1 onion, diced
2–3 carrots, diced
2 tablespoons extra virgin olive oil or vegetable oil
1.5 litres/6 cups vegetable stock

a handful of chopped fresh flat-leaf parsley (optional)
sea salt and black pepper
finely grated Parmesan-style vegetarian cheese, to serve

MAKES 4–6 SERVINGS

Put the stock in a saucepan and bring just to a simmer.

Combine the onion, carrots and oil in a separate saucepan and cook for 3–5 minutes, until soft. Add the barley and cook for 1 minute, stirring to coat all the grains in the oil. Season lightly. Add 2 ladlefuls of stock to the barley and cook, stirring constantly, until the liquid is absorbed. Continue adding the stock a ladleful at a time and stirring for about 30–40 minutes, until the barley is tender and most, if not all, of the stock has gone. Taste and adjust the seasoning.

Stir in the parsley (if using) and serve immediately with finely grated cheese.

A tried and tested recipe in my house, this one never fails to please. It is simplicity itself and this version is the simplest one in my repertoire, ideal for feeding all the family. It can be embellished with any number of ingredients: sautéed vegetables such as mushrooms or leeks, blanched kale or spinach, and enhanced by using a combination of other puréed root vegetables instead of all potato, such as turnip, parsnip, swede or celeriac.

mashed potato pie

1 kg/2 lbs. floury potatoes
30 g/2 tablespoons butter
1 egg, beaten
250 ml/1 cup milk
100 g/1½ cups grated vegetarian cheddar

150 g/1 cup frozen peas
sea salt and black pepper

a 23-cm/9-inch square baking dish, generously buttered

MAKES 6–8 SERVINGS

Halve the potatoes if large and put them in a large saucepan with sufficient cold water to cover well. (There is no need to peel them if they are organic.) Bring to the boil, then lower the heat and simmer gently for 20–25 minutes, until tender when pierced with a skewer.

Preheat the oven to 180ºC (350ºF) Gas 4.

Drain the potatoes and mash them well using a potato ricer or with a mashing tool. Transfer to a mixing bowl, stir in the butter and season well.

Whisk the egg and milk together in a small bowl and pour into the potatoes. Add 75 g/1 cup of the cheese and the peas and stir to blend.

Transfer to the prepared dish and spread evenly. Sprinkle over the remaining cheese and bake in the preheated oven for about 35–45 minutes, until golden. Serve immediately.

This recipe, vaguely modelled on stir-fried rice, offers a creative use for frozen mixed vegetables, which have to be a staple of family freezers the world over. It is healthful, tasty and quick to prepare. Chickpeas can be used in place of the cashews if preferred.

A very simple and speedy supper, which can be made from all storecupboard ingredients including frozen vegetables. If using fresh broccoli, use as much of the stems as possible to get the children used to eating more than just the floret.

curried rainbow rice with cashews

2 tablespoons vegetable oil

200 g/1 cup brown rice

1 small onion, diced

½ red (bell) pepper, diced

2 teaspoons mild curry powder

175 g/1 cup mixed diced frozen

vegetables (such as peas, sweetcorn, diced green beans etc), no need to defrost

150 g/1 cup cashews, left whole or coarsely chopped

MAKES 3–4 SERVINGS

Heat the oil in a large saucepan. Add the rice, onion, red pepper and curry powder. Cook for 2–3 minutes, stirring to coat in oil. Season lightly and add the vegetables and 600 ml/2⅓ cups water. Stir briefly just to mix, then bring to the boil. Without stirring again, lower the heat, cover with a lid and simmer over very low heat for 30–35 minutes, until the rice is tender and all the liquid has been absorbed. Stir well and serve hot or cold, as preferred.

sweet potato curry

1–2 tablespoons vegetable oil

1 large onion, finely chopped

2–4 teaspoons medium curry powder

1 tablespoon finely grated fresh ginger (optional)

500 g/1 lb. sweet potatoes, peeled and cubed

400-g/14-oz. can coconut milk

250 g/9 oz. broccoli florets

with long stems (fresh or frozen)

410-g/14-oz. can chickpeas

sea salt

cooked brown or white basmati rice, to serve

MAKES 3–4 SERVINGS

Heat the oil in a large saucepan and add the onion. Cook until soft. Stir in the curry powder and ginger and cook for 1–2 minutes more. Add the sweet potatoes and toss to coat in the oil. Add the coconut milk and simmer, uncovered, for about 15 minutes until the sweet potatoes are tender. Taste and adjust the seasoning. If using fresh broccoli, cook in boiling water for 3–5 minutes, until just tender, then drain before adding to the curry. If using frozen, add 15 minutes into cooking time and simmer until just tender.

Gently stir in the chickpeas and serve immediately with rice.

Variation Replace the broccoli with frozen whole leaf spinach or several handfuls of frozen peas and add a few minutes before the end of cooking time.

250-g/9-oz. tub ricotta

180 g/1½ cups chopped frozen spinach, defrosted

1 egg

4 tablespoons finely grated Parmesan-style vegetarian cheese

1 x 300-g/10½-oz. package fresh lasagne sheets (minimum 8 slices)

80–100 g/½–1 cup grated vegetarian cheddar

2 x 125-g/4½-oz. balls mozzarella, sliced

sea salt and black pepper

VEGETABLE BOLOGNESE

250 g/2½ cups coarsely chopped mushrooms

1 onion, coarsely chopped

1 carrot, coarsely chopped

1 small leek, washed

2 garlic cloves

1 celery stick, chopped

2–3 tablespoons extra virgin olive oil

1 teaspoon dried thyme (optional)

700 ml/2¾ cups passata (Italian sieved tomatoes)

400-g/14-oz. can chopped tomatoes

a pinch of sugar

1 dried bay leaf

sea salt and pepper

a 20 x 25 cm/8 x 10-inch lasagne dish or similar baking dish

MAKES 6–8 SERVINGS

Here is an indulgent supper dish all the family can enjoy. Putting the vegetables for the sauce in the food processor gives this vegetable-laden sauce a pleasing texture as well as disguising the fact that there a good few vegetables included.

three-cheese lasagne

To make the vegetable bolognese, put the mushrooms, onion, carrot, leek, garlic and celery in a food processor and process until very finely chopped. Transfer to a frying pan/skillet. Add the oil and thyme and cook over medium heat for 3–5 minutes, stirring often, until just beginning to brown. Add the passata, tomatoes, sugar and bay leaf. Stir to blend, then simmer, uncovered, for at least 15 minutes. Taste and season to taste.

Preheat the oven to 200ºC (400ºF) Gas 6.

Put the ricotta, spinach, egg, Parmesan-style cheese and a good pinch each of salt and pepper in a mixing bowl and whisk until thoroughly blended.

Spread a thin layer of the vegetable bolognese in the bottom of the lasagne dish and drizzle with a little olive oil. Top with 2 sheets of lasagne. Spread with just under one-third of the bolognese and top with 2 more lasagne sheets. Spread half of the ricotta mixture on top and sprinkle with half the grated cheddar. Top with 2 lasagne sheets then spread with one-third of the remaining bolognese. Top with 2 more lasagne sheets, spread over the remaining ricotta mixture and sprinkle over the remaining cheddar. Top with the remaining lasagne sheets and spread with a good layer of the bolognese.

Arrange the mozzarella slices on top and bake in the preheated oven for 30–40 minutes, until browned and bubbling. Serve hot with a salad.

Deliciously sweet roast pumpkin wedges work remarkably well with this mild chilli and rice dish. To spice this up for adults or for older children, add a generous dash of Tabasco and chopped fresh coriander/cilantro and serve with sour cream and sliced, pickled jalapeños, if liked.

veggie chilli with roast pumpkin wedges

1 tablespoon vegetable oil

1 onion, finely chopped

1 large carrot, finely chopped

1 green (bell) pepper, finely chopped

250 g/2½ cups finely chopped mushrooms

½ teaspoon chilli powder

1 teaspoon ground cumin

½ teaspoon allspice

½ teaspoon cayenne pepper (optional)

2 x 410-g/14-oz. cans kidney or pinto beans (or 1 of each), drained

400-g/14-oz. can chopped tomatoes

1 tablespoon ketchup

100 g/⅔ cup pitted black olives, halved (optional)

250 g/1 cup sweetcorn kernels, fresh or frozen

1 small pumpkin, seeded and cut into wedges

extra virgin olive oil, for roasting

sea salt and black pepper

cooked rice, to serve

MAKES 3–4 SERVINGS

Heat the oil in a large frying pan/skillet and add the onion, carrot, green pepper and mushrooms and cook for about 5 minutes, until soft. Season lightly and add the chilli powder, cumin, allspice and cayenne pepper (if using). Cook, stirring often, until browned.

Stir in the beans, tomatoes, ketchup, olives and sweetcorn and simmer gently, uncovered, for about 20–30 minutes, while the pumpkin roasts.

Preheat the oven to 200ºC (400ºF) Gas 6.

Arrange the pumpkin wedges on a baking sheet in a single layer. Coat generously with olive oil and sprinkle with salt. Roast in the preheated oven for about 30 minutes, until tender.

To serve, spoon the chilli and rice on the plates alongside a roast pumpkin wedge.

index